D0897866

The Marshall Plan

By Allen W. Dulles

This recently discovered study by Allen Dulles, brother of John Foster and Eleanor Dulles, OSS director in Switzerland during the Second World War and later director of the CIA, was written in the winter of 1947/48 when the acceptance of the Marshall Plan was still in doubt. At this point Dulles, who had been prominently involved in this recovery program, produced this well-argued and highly interesting manuscript forcefully putting the case for acceptance. However, his book offers not only fascinating insights into the dramatic atmosphere of the early postwar period, but may also serve as an inspiration to policymakers at a time when, forty-five years later, there is much discussion of recovery programs for Eastern Europe and the Marshall Plan is often evoked as a possible model.

Michael Wala, Assistant Professor at the Universität Erlangen-Nürnberg, is author of *Winning the Peace: Amerikanische Außenpolitik und der Council on Foreign Relations, 1945–1950* (1990).

Photo courtesy of Joan Dulles Buresch

The Marshall Plan

By Allen W. Dulles

Edited and with an Introduction by

Michael Wala

BERG
Providence / Oxford

Published in 1993 by

Berg Publishers, Inc.

Editorial offices:
165 Taber Avenue, Providence, RI 02906 U.S.A.
150 Cowley Road, Oxford OX4 1JJ, U.K.

©Michael Wala

**A CIP catalogue record for this book is available from
the British Library.**

Library of Congress Cataloging-in-Publication Data

Dulles, Allan Walsh. 1893–1932.
   The Marshall plan / by Allan W. Dulles : edited and with an
introduction by Michael Wala.
      p.   cm.   ⏄P
   Incudes index.
   ISBN 0–85496–350–2
   1. Marshall Plan.   2. Reconstruction (1939–1951)   3. Europe—
Foreign economic relations—United States.   4. United States—
Foreign economic relations—Europe.   I. Title.
HC240.D79   1992
338.9'17304—dc20   92–15793
                                                   CIP

Printed in the United States by E. B. Edwards Brothers, Ann Arbor, MI

Contents

Acknowledgments

The original manuscript of this book is located in the Allen W. Dulles Papers, box 36, Seeley G. Mudd Manuscript Library, Princeton University, Princeton, NJ. Ben Primer and Jean Holliday of that institution went out of their way to help in the project of publishing Dulles's study. I am very grateful for their help. Gabi Meyer, Sharon Mulak, and Olivier Szlos provided direly needed assistance in typing and proofreading. I am indebted to Allen W. Dulles's daughters, Mrs. Joan D. Buresch and Mrs. Clover D. Jebsen, the Dulles Committee, and the Princeton University Libraries for their permission to edit and publish the manuscript. They all provided highly appreciated help, support, and encouragement. Lastly, I would like to thank the George C. Marshall Foundation for its generous support.

M.W.

Editorial Note

The text has been corrected for obvious mistakes in orthography, quotations, dates, and misspelling of names. Dulles took most of the quotations from New York newspapers and other sources without identifying his sources. Footnotes have been added to indicate the paper, date, and page. In the few cases where Dulles had named his sources in the manuscript, this information has been transferred to a footnote. Notes numbered using asterisks are Dulles's original notes; notes numbered in arabic numbers are the editor's.

Preface

This volume by Allen Dulles was originally intended to be a part of the campaign to convince skeptical or hostile Americans that the European Recovery Program (called by everyone except George C. Marshall the "Marshall Plan") was a necessary and proper commitment of U.S. resources and prestige to foreign – and in some cases recent enemy – nations. Legislative approval for a large-scale foreign aid program seemed unlikely in 1947 and early 1948; Americans had already seen various bilateral aid agreements fail to solve the problems – problems that Americans, who had been safe from the war's devastation, tended to underestimate.

Secretary of State Marshall's speech at Harvard University on 5 June 1947 is frequently considered to be a nodal point in the early Cold War. Because the deepening economic crisis was clear to numerous observers, Marshall's speech had many fathers. Marshall recalled in 1959 that the date of the delivery was not accidental but carefully calculated. He had asked George F. Kennan and Charles Bohlen to work independently on ideas, and he dictated yet another version of his own. In the end, Marshall said, "I cut out part of Kennan's speech and part of Bohlen's speech and part of my speech and put the three together, and that was the beginning of the talk."

What Marshall took pride in, however, was selling the Marshall Plan to the American people and through them the Congress, not in enunciating the idea at Harvard. As with other kinds of planning, he later stated: "There's nothing so profound in the logic of the thing. But the execution of it, that's another matter. It's like our mobilization here [in 1940–41]. I flew thousands of miles a week, following through everything that happened in this country. ... I worked on that as hard as though I was running for the Senate or the presidency.... It was just a struggle from start to finish." He was particularly pleased with his success in converting Michigan Republican Arthur Vandenburg into an ardent supporter of the European Recovery Program.

The ultimate legislative success of the plan's supporters owed much to private groups such as the Committee for the Marshall Plan to Aid European Recovery, of which Allen Dulles was a founder – and of course to Soviet diplomacy. And while doctors of history and economics still debate the role and value to European political and economic recovery of the $13.3 billion, four-year program, the patient, so ill in 1947, has recovered magnificently and the operation has since become a popular synonym for success. On 10 December 1953, General Marshall received the Nobel Peace Prize for the Marshall Plan; he accepted it on behalf of the American people.

We at the Marshall Foundation are pleased to be associated with this important work and look forward to adding this important page of this country's history to the George C. Marshall Foundation's collection.

R. F. MARRYOTT
President and CEO
George C. Marshall Foundation

Introduction

Forty-five years ago, when the Marshall Plan was inaugurated, the European economies had been wrecked by World War II; today, the economies of Eastern Europe and the now independent republics of the former Soviet Union are ruined by the Cold War. After the collapse of COMECON and the disintegration of the Soviet Union, the economic deterioration in these countries has become the most crucial topic on the agenda of international economic problems. The task at hand is nothing less than the transformation of socialist, planned economies and their integration into the international system of capitalist, market economies. The fate of more than 400 million people is directly involved, and, considering the threatening potential of the means of mass destruction inherited from the Cold War, the future of the whole world might be at stake if these nations are overwhelmed by poverty, hunger, chaos, and desperation. The Marshall Plan has been mentioned, time and again, as an appropriate model and precedent for the vast undertaking that must be accomplished. Many politicians and commentators, it seems, regard the Marshall Plan as a panacea for all the economic, political, and social difficulties that have to be faced.

Although major disparities between the situation in which the original Marshall Plan was inaugurated in 1947/48 and the present crisis are obvious, there are also significant similarities. Clearly, the political arena is dramatically different today. In June 1947, the United States had political, strategic, and economic interests in helping the countries participating in the Marshall Plan. By stabilizing democratic institutions through economic aid and by urging close cooperation among the West European nations, American policy makers sought to prevent the Soviet Union from expanding its influence in Western Europe. The aid program also made it possible to utilize the work force and the skills of the former enemy Germany to help in the reconstruction of Western Europe while, simultaneously, keeping a possible resurgence of the German menace in check and rehabilitating Western Germany as a potential ally in the anticipated confrontation with the Soviet Union. Today, the Soviet Union has ceased to exit, and Germany has become an integral part of the Western economic and political system.

In 1947, the desperate economic situation in Europe had disrupted the system of international trade. Additionally, State Department officials were worried that the shift from war-time to peace-time economy might cause domestic economic problems. Facing a large export surplus, officials feared that the dwindling dollar reserves of the European nations and, thus, their inability to pay for imports, could easily spell unemployment and even a new depression for the United States. Today, despite occasional problems, a stable system of international trade relations exists.

Allen Welsh Dulles's analysis of the conditions in the late 1940s, despite all these differences, can help to focus the attention on essentials of economic aid for the East European nations and the independent republics of the former Soviet Union. His insistence that a closely coordinated effort would be necessary to assure the success of American aid should receive particular attention. Stressing that "exaggeration of national sovereignty has brought the capitalist world in Europe to the verge of ruin more than any one single factor" prior to World War II, Dulles warned that "the principle of self-determination, high and noble in itself, has dangerous implications in the economic field" (pages 3, 18). In addition to pointing out prerequisites for effective American aid and delineating the development of the Marshall Plan, Dulles thus also formulated general principles for economic aid that are as valid today as they were in 1947/48.

Allen Dulles is best – and in most cases only – known for his service as director of the Central Intelligence Agency (CIA) from 1953 to 1961. Those interested in the history of World War II may place him as the head of the Office of Strategic Services (the wartime American intelligence organization) in Switzerland, responsible for "Operation Sunrise," the surrender of the German forces in Italy. Hardly more than that is known about Dulles's personal history to the broader public, despite the fact that he is certainly not only a controversial figure but also one of the more interesting individuals of our time. Unfortunately, Dulles's concern for political matters and particularly his involvement in the activities to promote the Marshall Plan, of which his book on the Marshall Plan was an immediate result, have been widely neglected.[1]

Shortly after Secretary Marshall's speech at Harvard University, Dulles and many other interested individuals realized that the State Department would face severe difficulties in promoting the Marshall Plan. Arthur H. Vandenberg, chairperson of the Senate Committee on Foreign Affairs, expressed his doubts when, in response to a query by leading internationalist Clark M. Eichelberger, he wrote in June 1947, "I certainly do not take it for granted that the American public is ready for such burdens as would be involved" in providing assistance to Europe. This would remain a problem, he reflected, "until it is far more efficiently demonstrated to the American people that this (1) is in the latitude of their own available resources and (2) serves their intelligent self-interest."[2] Even before Marshall gave his speech, the heads of State Department offices discussed these issues at a meeting on 28 May 1947. Dean G. Acheson, then under secretary of state, pointed out that publicity for the aid plan would be necessary.[3]

Common ignorance of the general public and the dire state of public relations efforts during the following months were difficult problems, indeed, for the State Department. Concern that the department alone would not be able to conduct a sufficiently influential campaign for the support of economic aid to Europe was rapidly growing in internationalist circles and even among officials at the State Department.

---

1. There is no biography of Allen Dulles yet available, though the gap will hopefully be filled by the forthcoming *Gentleman Spy: The Lives of Allen Welsh Dulles*, by Peter Grose, executive editor of *Foreign Affairs*, working with R. Harris Smith, to be published in the United States by Houghton Mifflin. A rather superficial and not always reliable biography of the Dulles family is Leonard Mosley, *Dulles: A Biography of Eleanor, Allen, and John Foster Dulles and Their Family Network* (New York, 1978). Dulles's own book, *The Craft of Intelligence* (New York, 1963), written in his retirement, contains some biographical information as "A Personal Note," pp. 1–5.

2. Eichelberger to Vandenberg, 24 June 1947, Clark M. Eichelberger Papers, box 20, New York Public Library, New York; Vandenberg to Eichelberger, 25 June 1947, ibid. This letter is also cited in Arthur H. Vandenberg, Jr., ed., *The Private Papers of Senator Vandenberg* (Boston, 1952) 381. Eichelberger had been a pivotal force in the creation of the pre–Pearl Harbor Committee to Defend America and held leading positions in a number of internationalist organizations such as the American Association for the United Nations (AAUN). See his autobiography *Organizing for Peace: A Personal History of the Founding of the United Nations* (New York, 1977) and Michael Wala, "Selling War and Selling Peace: The Non-Partisan Committee for Peace, the Committee to Defend America, and the Committee for the Marshall Plan," *Amerikastudien/American Studies* 30 (Fall 1985): 91–105.

3. "Summary of Discussion on Problems of Relief, Rehabilitation and Reconstruction of Europe," dated 28 May 1947, reprinted in U.S. Department of State, *Foreign Relations of the United States, 1947* (Washington, D.C., 1972) 3: 235 (hereafter abbreviated as *FRUS, 1947*). See also Charles E. Bohlen, *Witness to History, 1929–69* (New York, 1973) 264.

By September, the department had still not taken any decisive actions, and interests outside the government became increasingly aware that the existing information process was insufficient. Assistant Secretary of State for Public Affairs William Benton wrote to Secretary Marshall and Acheson's successor, Under Secretary Robert M. Lovett, on 19 September that "sharp criticism from the public – both from political and other leaders, and from the press – saying that the government is not supplying the necessary information to obtain understanding of the European economic crisis" was being raised with increasing frequency. Opinion polls, he continued, "indicate that only an insignificant minority of the American people have the remotest understanding of the 'Marshall proposal,' let alone have heard of it."[4] Members of a Council on Foreign Relations study group on "Public Opinion and Foreign Policy" were informed in a similar fashion. State Department officials who took part in a study group meeting admitted that "*planned* public relations" work had ceased and that the Department was in a state of "confusion regarding the Marshall Plan."[5]

Efforts supporting the Marshall Plan received another blow when William Benton resigned from his post to run for the U.S. Senate, thus leaving the State Department without leadership when coordinated publicity work for the Marshall Plan was direly needed. Eager to find a suitable candidate with excellent ties to the "interested public" to replace Benton, Lovett offered the post to a number of individuals, including Allen Dulles. To the disappointment of Lovett, Dulles declined the bid, claiming inexperience in the field of public relations.[6]

However, by that time, when he was declining Lovett's offer, Dulles was actually already deeply engaged in the activities promoting the Marshall Plan. In early August 1947, Christian A. Herter (Republican, Massachusetts), vice-chairman of the House Select Committee on Foreign Aid, had asked Dulles to serve as a consultant for the committee. Herter had proposed the establish-

4. Office Memorandum, "Subject: Information Program Concerning European Reconstruction Problem," Benton to Lovett and Secretary Marshall, 19 September 1947, box 3, Records of the Assistant Secretary of State for Public Affairs, National Archives, Record Group 59, Washington, D.C. (ASPA).

5. Digest of Discussion (DD), 25 September 1947, study group on "Public Opinion and Foreign Policy," Records of Groups (RG) XVIIIA, Council on Foreign Relations Archives (hereafter abbreviated as RGCFR with the appropriate volume number), Harold Pratt House, New York. The emphasis is in the original.

6. Dulles to Lovett, 26 November 1947, *personal* and *confidential*, Dulles Papers, box 30. Dulles makes a reference to a telephone call by Lovett the previous day. Dulles had not been Lovett's first choice.

ment of the committee on 15 July (House of Representatives, Resolution 296, 80th Congress); and, soon after its creation, the members went on a fact-finding tour to Europe. After their return, the committee produced twenty-four preliminary reports in addition to a final report. Dulles's major input in these activities was with the preliminary report delineating the legal and administrative phases of the aid program, interests that are reflected in his book on the Marshall Plan.[7]

In addition to this work, Dulles concurrently became a founding member of an organization solely created to do public relations work on behalf of the aid program: the Committee for the Marshall Plan to Aid European Recovery, chaired by Henry L. Stimson, the former secretary of war. The committee had been created at the suggestion of Clark Eichelberger and Alger Hiss. Hiss – better known today for his trial and conviction for perjury – had been a member of the Council study group "Public Opinion and Foreign Policy" and had just been appointed president of the Carnegie Endowment for International Peace. Until recently an official in the State Department, he contacted his former associates and staff members from the office of Under Secretary of State for Economic Affairs William L. Clayton.[8]

Eichelberger and Hiss approached former Secretary of War Robert P. Patterson with their proposal to form a citizens' committee for the Marshall Plan on 1 October 1947. They could tell Patterson that government officials would be grateful for the support. The next day Patterson called Lovett for his views because of a need to be personally reassured of the State Department's approval. Lovett replied favorably, confirming that such an action would be most welcome. Contacting Secretary of Commerce W. Averell Harriman, Patterson received an equally positive response.[9]

7. Herter to Dulles, 4 August 1947, Dulles Papers, box 30; Charles A. Eaton to Dulles, 8 August 1947, Dulles Papers, box 29. See also "Statement by Allen Welsh Dulles, February 24, 1948, Committee on Foreign Relations, House of Representatives," n.d., Dulles Papers, box 36. The records of the Select Committee on Foreign Aid are located at the National Archives, Washington, D.C. Only a very minor and insignificant part of the records had been processed and made available to scholars as of fall 1990.

8. Hiss to Eichelberger, 6 October 1947, Carnegie Endowment for International Peace Records (CEIPR), no. 63652, Butler Library, Columbia University, New York. For a more extensive account of the committee's activities, see Michael Wala, "Selling the Marshall Plan at Home: The Committee for the Marshall Plan to Aid European Recovery," *Diplomatic History* 10 (Summer 1986): 247–65.

9. Memorandum, Eichelberger to Robert P. Patterson, 3 October 1947, Patterson Papers, box 41, Library of Congress, Washington, D.C.; Patterson to Stimson, 16 October 1947, ibid., Robert M. Lovett, Daily Log and Diary, entry of 2 October 1947, Brown Brothers, Harriman, and Co. Records, New York Historical Society, New York.

Introduction

At an initial gathering on 30 October 1947, the committee members agreed to place full-page advertisements in the national press, such as the *New York Times*, the New York *Herald Tribune*, and the *Washington Post*.[10] The committee established its headquarters in New York City and, to stay in touch with events on Capitol Hill, opened an office in Washington, D.C. Along the East Coast, chapters (often led by prominent citizens) were formed quickly. During the five months the committee was operational, more than $162 thousand in donations was received. Promotion and publicity costs totaled $24 thousand and expenditures for telephone calls and telegrams took another $11 thousand. Nearly $60 thousand of the total amount went into publication and distribution of more than 1.25 million copies of a variety of printed materials.[11]

The committee calculated its publication and distribution strategy to correspond with the needs of different sections of the population. Since the public at large maintained a negative position toward the Marshall Plan as a means of anti-Soviet policy, information directed at it followed opinion polls and emphasized the humanitarian aspects of the program and the benefits the Marshall Plan would have for the United States' domestic economy.[12] A different approach was used for the members of the foreign policy establishment. According to a poll conducted by the Council on Foreign Relations, a majority was convinced that

> [w]hile the Secretary's address, from which 'the Marshall Plan' has stemmed, was a statesmanlike utterance, his observation that 'our policy is directed not against any country or doctrine,' should not be taken

10. Memorandum, Clark M. Eichelberger, dated 30 October 1947, Committee for the Marshall Plan, Files and Minutes (CMPR), box 2, Harry S. Truman Library, Independence, MO; "Suggested Activities of the Citizens Committee to Support the Marshall Plan," n.d., enclosure to public relations counsel Harold Oram to Executive Committee Members, 31 October 1947, Winthrop W. Aldrich Papers, box 105, Baker Library, Harvard University, Cambridge, Massachusetts.
11. Minutes of Meeting, 26 November 1947, CMPR, box 2. Letterheads of the local chapters can be found in the Patterson Papers, box 41. See also John H. Ferguson, *Report on the Activities of the Committee for the Marshall Plan to Aid European Recovery* (New York, n.d.) 2, 7. For the amounts mentioned, see "Receipt and Disbursement Statement," Haskins & Sells to Committee of the Marshall Plan, 30 August 1948, CMPR, box 1; Form A, Lobbying Act, n.d., ibid.; Form A, Lobbying Act, April 1948, ibid.; Form A, Lobbying Act, 8 January 1948, ibid.; see also ledgers, ibid. Of the members of the executive committee of the Committee for the Marshall Plan, sixteen were members of the Council on Foreign Relations, five of these sat on the board of the Woodrow Wilson Foundation, and four were members of the AAUN. The National Council had more than two hundred members from throughout the nation.
12. Polls conducted until the end of 1947 by the American Institute of Public Opinion (Gallup) are summarized in *Public Opinion Quarterly* (Winter 1947/48): 675–76.

at face value at the present time. American policy is, and should be, directed against Communism.

Accordingly, this group primarily received publications which emphasized the anti-Soviet potential of the recovery program Dulles had stressed and which accentuated the program as a part of America's containment policy.[13]

The committee achieved its most direct influence in promoting the Marshall Plan, however, not by printing and distributing leaflets and booklets, but by providing and briefing witnesses for Senate and House hearings on foreign aid. A few committee members appeared as representatives of the committee, others as representatives of the business community or of various other interest groups, and Allen Dulles testified as a staff member of the House Select Committee on Foreign Aid. He was convinced, he said at that occasion, "that an effective European Recovery Program is essential to American security." The committee did not provide these witnesses only of its own accord but also because Marshall Plan supporters in Congress and State Department officials asked the committee to do so. Senator Vandenberg had urged Robert Lovett in a letter on 10 December 1947 to enlist "four or five top-level business executives as...aggressive witnesses" to appear before the Senate Committee on Foreign Relations. In response, Lovett had contacted Patterson. Since Patterson was in Washington at the time, Lovett dictated Vandenberg's confidential letter over the phone to Patterson's secretary, inquiring whether Patterson could not help in finding "four or five...powerful advocates from business...so that we can get them well briefed."[14]

The Committee for the Marshall Plan, created to sell the Marshall Plan to a reluctant public and a skeptical Congress, represented the most explicit attempt to shape public opinion during the beginning Cold War. Energetically, persuasively, and intelli-

13. See the synopsis of the poll conducted among members of the local chapters of the Council on Foreign Relations, the Committees on Foreign Relations, at the end of 1947 in Joseph Barber, ed., *The Marshall Plan as American Policy: A Report on the Views of Community Leaders in 21 Cities* (New York, 1948) 4.

14. "Statement by Allen Welsh Dulles," 1; Minutes of Meeting, 11 December 1947, CMPR, box 2; Vandenberg to Lovett, 10 December 1947, cited in Susan M. Hartman, *Truman and the 80th Congress* (Columbia, MO, 1971) 160; Lovett Daily Log and Diary, entry of 11 December 1947. A list of possible experts for Congressional hearings is added to the Office Memorandum, Acting Legislative Counsel Carl Marcey to the Assistant Secretary of State for Economic Affairs Dallas W. Dort, 31 December 1947, State Department, Decimal File 840.50, National Archives, RG 59. Almost all experts listed were committee members.

gently, using lobbying, advertisements, and business strategies – skills which they knew and employed in their careers as managers and lawyers – Dulles and the other committee members accomplished their envisioned goal and induced Congress to believe that the American people overwhelmingly supported Marshall's initiative.[15]

The Marshall Plan was by no means Allen Dulles's first encounter with diplomacy. As with his more famous older brother, John Foster Dulles, Allen Dulles's interest in politics and international affairs was already well developed in his childhood. It was nurtured by his grandfather, John W. Foster, who had been secretary of state in 1892 and 1893 under Benjamin Harrison, and by his uncle, Robert Lansing, secretary of state under Woodrow Wilson.[16]

After graduating from Princeton University in 1914, Dulles travelled around the world, teaching English for a year at Allahabad, India. Returning to the United States in 1915, he went back to Princeton to receive his master's degree in 1916. With his interest in world affairs not having subsided – the law he had studied would never really become a lifetime devotion – Dulles decided to enter the diplomatic service. The United States was not yet a belligerent in World War I; thus he was appointed secretary to the U.S. embassy in Vienna, Austria, in May 1916. After President Wilson declared war on Germany, on 6 April 1917, Dulles was transferred to Bern, Switzerland. It was here that he first came into contact with the craft of intelligence, an occupation that was to remain his leading concern for the rest of his life.

After Germany had signed the cease-fire agreement at Compiègne, France, on 11 November 1918, Dulles became a member of the American delegation to the Paris Peace Conference at Versailles and there took part in the commission that determined the boundaries of the newly created nation of Czechoslovakia. At the end of 1919, he was among the personnel to open the first postwar American mission in Berlin. On 15

15. Actually, when the American Institute for Public Opinion surveyed citizens' views on the Marshall Plan in March 1947, it found that still not more than 45 percent of the general public supported aid to Europe. See *Public Opinion Quarterly*, 12 (Summer 1948): 365.

16. In addition to standard sources, biographical data are taken from Dulles, "A Personal Note"; and "Allen Welsh Dulles: Author of 'Germany's Underground,'" n.d., Dulles Papers, box 31; "Author's Publicity Questionnaire: Trade Department, the Macmillan Company," dated 4 February 1947, Dulles Papers, box 28. This form was used for Dulles's book *Germany's Underground* (New York, 1947). Lansing was the son-in-law of John W. Foster.

October 1920, he was assigned to duty with the American High Commission in Constantinople, Turkey (today's Istanbul). Back in Washington, D.C., he was designated chief of the Division of Near Eastern Affairs of the State Department in April 1922. Interrupted by an assignment to be a delegate to represent the United States at the International Conference on the Traffic in Arms, in May 1925 in Geneva, and to act as a member of the Preparatory Commission on the Limitations of Armaments in 1926, he served in his position at the State Department until his retirement from the diplomatic service on 15 October 1926.

Having "exhausted" his "exchequer" and persuaded by his older brother John Foster to give up diplomacy for law, Allen Dulles reluctantly entered the law firm of Sullivan & Cromwell, of which John Foster Dulles was by then a senior partner. His stint at law was repeatedly interrupted by government assignments: as legal adviser to the American Delegation to the Three Power Naval Conference at Geneva (1927), and as legal adviser to the American Delegation at the General Disarmament Conference at Geneva (1932–1933). In 1941 he went on a special mission for the American government to Bolivia to remove the German influence and control from airlines in that country.

Shortly after Japanese forces attacked the American Pacific Fleet at Pearl Harbor, William J. Donovan asked Dulles to join the newly established Office of Strategic Services (OSS). In November 1942 Dulles was sent to neutral Switzerland to conduct intelligence operations on Germany from his station in Bern. His greatest success during that time was "Operation Sunrise," the surrender of the German forces in Italy on 28 April 1945.[17]

Negotiations between emissaries of SS General Karl Wolff and Dulles had already begun two months earlier but had been hampered in early April by Russian demands to be involved in the talks and by accusations that Great Britain and the United States were scheming for a separate peace with Germany. After President Roosevelt died on 12 April 1945, Dulles was ordered to discontinue his contact with the Germans. The SS General – cynically expressing his "sincere and deeply felt condolences" with the "highest respect for the majesty of death" – had anticipated difficulties and wrote to Dulles that he feared the negotiations might

---

17. For a short overview of the range of OSS activities, see Lawrence H. McDonald, "The Office of Strategic Services: America's First National Intelligence Agency," *Prologue* 23 (Spring 1991): 7–22.

be thwarted. With the Germans set on the course of capitulation, however, Truman finally decided to accept the surrender.[18]

Immediately after Germany's unconditional capitulation on 8 May 1945, Dulles established the OSS mission in Germany and served as its chief until August 1945. At that time Dulles probably still believed in the possibility of a continuation of war-time cooperation with the Soviet Union, even after his frustrating experience with Soviet misgivings about his negotiations with Wolff in Switzerland. However, in Germany, he was repeatedly hindered in the conduct of his work by Soviet colleagues and became quite disillusioned. Americans could hardly move freely in the Soviet zone of occupation and to their dismay discovered that many moderate German socialists returning to their homes in Eastern Germany disappeared. This meant, quite possibly, that they were either killed or sent to Siberia.

Frustrated with this experience and enlightened by his first-hand encounter with Soviet occupational policy, he went back to New York to practice law again at Sullivan & Cromwell. This did not, however, mean that he did not any longer pursue his interests in world affairs. Within a short time he became president of the Near East Colleges Association, director of the Woodrow Wilson Foundation, and chairperson of the Committee on International Law of the New York County Lawyer's Association. As legal adviser for the Interim Committee on Headquarters of the United Nations, he helped to establish the United Nations in New York City; and, in November 1946, he was elected president of the most prestigious foreign policy organization, the New York-based Council on Foreign Relations.[19]

---

18. Wolff had coyly crossed out his letterhead introducing him as "SS-Obergruppenführer and General of the Waffen-SS, Highest SS- and Police-Leader and Authorized General of the German Forces in Italy." See Wolff to Dulles, 15 April 1945, Dulles Papers, box 22. My translation from the original German. Dulles's own account of "Operation Sunrise" is in his *Secret Surrender* (New York, 1966).

19. The Council on Foreign Relations had been founded in 1921 through the merger of an "old" council (created in 1918 in New York City by a group of businessmen) with the American Institute of International Affairs. The latter organization was established in Paris in 1919 by members of the American delegation to the peace conference as a counterpart of what today is known as the Royal Institute for International Affairs in London. Dulles, although at that time in Paris, had not been involved in these activities. See Whitney H. Shepardson, *Early History of the Council on Foreign Relations* (Stamford, CT, 1960), Robert D. Schulzinger *The Wise Men of Foreign Affairs: The History of the Council on Foreign Relations* (New York, 1984), and Michael Wala, *Winning the Peace: Amerikanische Außenpolitik und der Council on Foreign Relations, 1945–1950* (Stuttgart, 1990).

Dulles's association with the Council on Foreign Relations had deep roots. In 1927 he had become a director of the council, and from 1933 until 1944 he was its secretary. He was one of the original members of the War and Peace Studies project the council conducted in close cooperation with the Department of State from September 1939 until V-J Day. In the heated political atmosphere after Nazi Germany's attack on Poland and the subsequent declarations of war against Germany by Great Britain and France, State Department officials hardly had time to think ahead of their daily chores in order to develop long-range plans and a future foreign policy strategy for the United States. The council's proposal to help out in this matter received a warm welcome. Until August 1945, when the project was terminated, this program resulted in more than six hundred memoranda for the State Department, some of which had a direct and immediate impact on American foreign policy. As rapporteur, Dulles had chaired the "Security and Armaments Group" of the program. Scarcely three months after his arrival in New York in 1945, Dulles once again was engaged in the council's activities and chaired a study group on the political and economic situation in Western Europe.[20]

Earlier than many of his peers in the United States, Dulles had concluded that Germany was at the focal point of a number of important decisions determining the future political, strategic, and economic situation of Europe and consequently of the postwar world. Germany was vitally important for European economic restoration, and it was the site where the future predominance of the Soviet or of the American economic and political systems in Europe would be determined.

Dulles was certain that clashes between the USSR and the U.S. were almost inevitable and only "insulating the two systems" promised a chance for a lasting peace. The European infrastructure of roads, railroads, and waterways had been nearly totally destroyed by the war. "Europe as a whole," Dulles reminded the group members, "cannot get back to anything like normal condi-

---

20. For the War and Peace Studies, see Laurence H. Shoup and William Minter, *Imperial Brain Trust: The Council on Foreign Relations & United States Foreign Policy* (New York, 1977). Official accounts are Council on Foreign Relations, *The War and Peace Studies of the Council on Foreign Relations* (New York, 1946), and U.S. Department of State, *Postwar Foreign Policy Preparations, 1939-1945* (Washington, D.C., 1949), Harley Notter ed. Dulles served in this position until June 1940, and after that date together with Hanson W. Baldwin (naval and military editor of the *New York Times*) until December 1943. He had also become a member of the program's "Steering Committee" until that date.

tions, not to speak of prosperity, with a completely disorganized Germany."[21]

The discussion at a group meeting on 28 May 1946 turned out to be almost a nucleus of the future American policy in Europe. European reconstruction, it was maintained, was important to the fabric of international economic ties and to the well-being of the United States. A speedy and effective restoration of the European economies depended upon German economic rehabilitation, which in turn was only achievable if Germany were treated as an economic unit. Russia, however, was preventing that very thing from occurring. The division of Germany was a fact, members stated, and a West European federation, including the three western zones of Germany, should be established. Asked if this would not violate the Potsdam agreements, the council members were informed by Dulles that, if unification of Germany was offered "to Russia and she turned it down, then Russia and not the United States would be in the position of rejecting the Potsdam formula." He suggested "offer[ing] the Soviets a feasible plan," but in the event that the Soviets did not accept it, the United States should "work out a constructive policy for western Germany."[22]

More than three months before the United States offered economic unity with other zones of occupation in July 1946, Dulles's group had thus advocated unification of the three western zones of Germany; and, long before Secretary of State Byrnes's well-known Stuttgart speech in September 1946, it called for a strong revitalization of German industry. Under Dulles's chairmanship, the study group was also utilized to disseminate the conviction among a broader public, that economic reconstruction of Germany was imperative and only the degree of rehabilitation was up for debate. Undoubtedly, Dulles, like many of his peers in the government, was convinced that Germany had to be prevented from ever again being able to attack its neighbors. Germany, nevertheless, had to be put back to work to help in the rehabilitation of the European economy as a whole.[23]

The future treatment of Germany and restoration of the European economies, Dulles knew quite well, had to be at the core of foreign policy decision making. This would force decisions upon the American government which would inevitably lead to

---

21. "Memorandum for J.F.D. [John Foster Dulles]," dated 14 May 1946, John F. Dulles Papers, box 28, Seeley G. Mudd Manuscript Library, Princeton University, Princeton, NJ. Manuscript "Talk at CFR, 12/3/45," Allen Dulles Papers, box 21.

22. DD, 28 March 1946, 3–4, study group on "Western European Affairs" (WEA), RGCFR-XVIIIE.

23. The findings of the study group were summarized by Dulles in his article "Alternatives for Germany," *Foreign Affairs* 25 (Fall 1947): 421–32.

discord with the Soviet Union. Accordingly, when Secretary of State George C. Marshall returned disappointed from the foreign minister's conference at Moscow in late April 1947, the State Department machinery was put into gear to formulate plans to implement an American aid program, a program of "political economy in the literal sense of that term," as George F. Kennan was to call it later.[24]

In line with his previous activities at the Council on Foreign Relations, Dulles was very much concerned that the Marshall Plan be enacted successfully and speedily. When he returned from a trip to Europe just four days after Marshall gave his famous speech at Harvard University on 5 June 1947, Dulles wrote that he came "back from Europe with a very sobering view of the state of the world and of the immense responsibility which rests on the United States. Personally," he continued, "I do not feel that there was ever a time, even in the dark days of 1917 and 1940, when more depended upon what the United States is prepared to do."[25]

Dulles met Marshall personally only a few days later, on 16 June. Both had been invited to receive honorary degrees at Brown University. Here, Dulles elaborated on his endorsement of the still nascent recovery plan for Europe. Delineating the economic situation in Great Britain, France, Italy, the Netherlands, and the other West European countries, he expressed his belief that "it is by restoring the economic life of a country, and by this alone, that we can meet the threat of dictatorship from a Fascist Right or a Communist Left." Whereas Secretary Marshall had been rather subdued in addressing the target of the proposed aid program, Dulles was quite outspoken. If the United States would concentrate aid "on those countries with free institutions," the "common cause of democracy and peace" would be promoted. "We would thus," Dulles pointed out, "confront Communism, not with arms or atomic bombs, but with a restored economic life for the men and women of Western Europe."[26]

It was in this setting that Dulles wrote his book on the Marshall Plan. Almost ready to be submitted to a publisher in January 1948, its purpose was to help to convince an interested public that the Marshall Plan was important to the interests of the United States

24. "The Director of the Policy Planning Staff (Kennan) to the Under Secretary of State (Acheson)," dated 23 May 1947, reprinted in *FRUS, 1947*, 3: 230.

25. Dulles to Norman Armour, 10 June 1947, Dulles Papers, box 28.

26. Dulles, "Address to the Annual Meeting of the Associated Alumni of Brown University, 179th Annual Commencement, June 16, 1947," 7, 12. A copy of the printed version is in the Dulles Papers, box 30. Marshall had left shortly after he had been awarded the honorary degree (and before Dulles's speech) to attend to urgent matters in Washington.

and that Congress should pass the necessary legislation and make appropriations as speedily as possible. Dulles believed that if the American public knew and understood all the facts about the situation in Europe and the possibilities the Marshall Plan offered, even the last critic would be convinced.[27]

As a result of developments in Europe, with a coup in Czechoslovakia as the major factor, however, the European Recovery Program was enacted by Congress much faster than many had hoped, and too fast for the publication of Dulles's book. With the unexpectedly smooth passage of the Foreign Aid Act in March and April 1948, the book could no longer serve the purpose it was intended for if it was to be published as it had been written in early January 1948. Dulles' duties as president of the Council on Foreign Relations, his responsibilities at Sullivan & Cromwell, and his membership on the "Committee of Three," shaping the newly created Central Intelligence Agency, prevented him from rewriting the book.

Today, this book is a valuable source for an understanding of the European Recovery Program, written by an individual immediately concerned and involved. It is not so much an historical account of the implementation of the Marshall Plan, but rather a delineation of the developments that led to its formation and a strong argument for its implementation. It is quite obvious that Dulles saw the larger implications of the recovery program, when he wrote that it

> is not a philanthropic enterprise....It is based on our views of the requirements of American security....This is the only peaceful avenue now open to us which may answer the communist challenge to our way of life and our national security (page 116).

Dulles' study thus sheds light on the reasoning and arguments advanced by a very large sector of the attentive "foreign policy public," and it provides an insight into the general principles of foreign aid.

M.W.

Stanford
January 1992

27. Until April 1948, Allen Dulles gave more than seven speeches or papers on behalf of the Marshall Plan. Among them were appearances at the 9th District Republican Club (23 January 1948), the Export Managers Club, New York (6 January 1948), the Junior Investment Bankers and Brokers Association of New York, the National Association of Manufacturers, the National Republican Club, People's Platform over CBS on 23 November 1947, and the Pleasantville Community Forum in New York (16 February 1948). All manuscripts can be found in the Allen Dulles Papers.

We Must Choose a Course

The year 1948 will be a year of great debate on American foreign policy. In some respects this debate will resemble that of 1919 over the Treaty of Versailles and the League of Nations. At that time, emerging from a great war and following a great victory, we were faced with a decision whether or not to build on that victory and make common cause with our Allies in organizing the peace. We turned aside from that course and decided to go our own way.

Twenty years later we had good cause to regret our action. We found to our cost that those to whom we had left the primary responsibility to organize Europe did not have the resources equal to the task. They were unable to check a vengeful and ambitious Germany from starting on a course of conquest.

Today we face the decision as to whether, after a second great victory in a war fought to prevent Europe and Asia from being dominated by powers hostile to us, we now propose to leave Western Europe, and by implication Asia also, unaided in the face of a similar threat. Today it is the Soviet dictatorship which is on the move, and we need hardly delude ourselves with the idea, as we did in 1919, that the powers friendly to us, either in Europe or in Asia, have the strength, unaided, to meet that threat.

The issues will be debated by the country and by the Congress. The essence of the Marshall Plan is that we should meet the challenge by economic means; by helping to restore the economies of the countries of Western Europe and eventually, we hope, also of China. In the Pacific area, as the year 1948 opened, there was as yet no concrete program. We seemed to be at a loss to know what to do to help our Chinese ally.

As regards Europe the situation is different. There, a plan of action had been formulated and presented. The American people now have to decide what they wish to do about it. In making this decision the ultimate security and well-being of the United States – not that of other powers – is the prime consideration.

Anyone who visited Europe in the late spring or early summer of 1947 came away with serious forebodings. The pump priming which the United States had done for a very sick Continent was coming to an end, as Europe, emerging from the worst winter in decades, was facing the most devastating drought of recent times. The European economic crisis was not, as we had hoped, behind us – it was looming threateningly ahead of us. Europe, in fact, was being driven back to its economic beachheads. It was not only dollars and food and supplies which were running out – hope and faith in a future were dwindling too. Something had started which was in the nature of an economic run on the European bank of resources, and slender resources they were in that year 1947. Action was needed and needed promptly to turn the tide.

It was under these circumstances that on the 5th of June 1947 General George C. Marshall, secretary of state, went to the Harvard graduation exercise to accept the degree of Doctor of Laws. He took the opportunity to make a few remarks. After describing the shattered condition of Europe, he referred briefly to American assistance generously given, and then said, "before the United States Government can proceed much further in its efforts to alleviate the situation and help start the European world on its way to recovery, there must be some agreement among the countries of Europe as to the requirements of the situation and the part those countries themselves will take in order to give proper effect to whatever action might be undertaken by this Government.... *The initiative, I think, must come from Europe.*"[1]

Here was a ray of hope, and Europe reacted quickly. In fact, the implications of the Marshall speech were appreciated abroad before they were recognized here in the United States. Ernest Bevin, the British foreign minister,[2] was off to Paris. After consultation with Georges Bidault, the French foreign minister,[3] Moscow was consulted, refused to have anything to do with the proposal and directed its satellites to join in this refusal.[4] Nevertheless, the nations of Western Europe went ahead.

1. Marshall's speech is reprinted in *FRUS, 1947*, 3: 237–39. Emphasis is Dulles's.
2. Ernest Bevin served as British foreign minister from 1945 until 1951.
3. Ernest Bidault, after serving as French foreign minister from 1947 to 1948, became defense minister. He again was foreign minister from 1953 to 1954.
4. Actually, Poland and Czechoslovakia had indicated that they would be interested to participate. Czechoslovakia had accepted the invitation to attend the conference scheduled for 12 July Dulles mentions below on 8 July, but declined only two days later on 10 July.

In reply to invitations sent to most of the Continental states, the representatives of sixteen governments met in Paris on July 12 to see what they could do about the Marshall offer.[5] It was called a "plan," but, in truth, there was no plan. The phrase was an expression of attitude and intent. It meant simply that if the European governments could get together, could pool their energies and resources, the United States government would see what it could do toward helping them.

Meanwhile, the Russians went their way with the Molotov Plan, which simply meant that there would be no pooling of the resources of Eastern Europe with those of Western Europe if Russia could help it.[6] At one and the same moment the Russians were afraid of military encirclement, strong in their determination to expand both their territory and their influence, arrogant in their doctrinaire conviction that in Marx they had a full set of answers for the future and a method to guide them, and maddeningly sensitive because, after thirty years of attempting to install a Communist economy that same economy still worked with a clank, a lurch, and a stumble. This state of mind discloses one reason for the Soviet leaders' attitude toward the Marshall Plan. They are afraid of how they will look if the Plan succeeds. So, while indeed they would agree with the late Wendell Willkie that it is *One World*[7] – provided it is a Communist world – the Russians actually are the most intransigent insisters upon national sovereignty so long as the capitalist nations stay in business.

The exaggeration of national sovereignty has brought the capitalist world in Europe to the verge of ruin more than any one single factor. The Soviets see this and have good reason to believe that if they can keep the old idea of sovereignty alive they will profit. Hence, we Americans would like to see the Europeans devise a customs union, erase trade barriers, and do everything possible to permit goods to move freely about the Continent and

5. These nations were Austria, Belgium, Denmark, France, Greece, Iceland, Eire, Italy, Luxembourg, the Netherlands, Norway, Portugal, Sweden, Switzerland, Turkey, United Kingdom.

6. The Molotov Plan, named after the Soviet foreign minister, was hardly more than a series of restrictive trade agreements between the USSR and East European countries designed to bind those nations more strongly to the USSR and to prevent diversion of resources to help in the Marshall Plan countries.

7. *One World* had been the title of a the best-selling book prominent Republican Wendell Willkie had published at the end of 1942 after visiting the Soviet Union and China. Inspired by a faith in a better and peaceful future and believing in the goodwill of all human beings, Willkie had imagined a unifying force that would bring about freedom and justice for all of mankind. Within a short time, his book had sold more than one million copies.

thus utilize to the full the resources they have. The Russians insist on keeping up the barriers.

The Soviet Union does not want war with the United States. This I firmly believe. The cost of wars in terms of devastation and exhaustion, of manpower and munitions, has become so great that governments everywhere tremble at the thought of another. But the Russians, by every means short of war, will exert themselves to destroy the capitalist system in Europe and hence to win this particular contest now going on. So the cold war of maneuver and pressure continues.

When Secretary Marshall made his offer to Europe last June, he knew well enough that the gesture was worthless unless it was backed up by Congress, and that it would not be backed by Congress unless the people understood and approved. An American president or his secretary of state cannot give away either money or American assets unless Congress votes to do so and supplies the wherewithal. Messrs. Stalin or Molotov, on the contrary, could announce the Russian decision with finality. When the little group which runs the Soviet Union wants to initiate a policy or change its mind, it does not need to consult a Congress.

As Congress meets in Washington to decide what it will do about the Marshall Plan,[8] the Communist forces in both Italy and France – through riots, strikes, and disturbance generally – are attempting to throw Western Europe into such a turmoil that economic recovery will be impossible. They also hope to "scare" the United States away from embarking on a "hopeless" enterprise. As this country was taking the first step forward by approving interim aid of $548 million on December 17, 1947, the Communists were suffering their greatest setbacks in France and Italy.[9]

But the major decision of policy remains to be made on the long-range European Recovery Program. That decision will govern the course of our foreign policy for many years. It may determine whether the United States will emerge from the postwar period isolated in the face of the great power of Russia, or whether it will stand secure, working with strong allies to keep the peace.

8. The manuscript reads "it will do about (the) Marshall̶s̶(Plan) expression of intent, the communist forces ..." (where — indicates deleted sections and ( ) indicates an insertion). It is obvious that the words "expression of intent," should also have been deleted.

9. Interim Aid was provided by the appropriations for the Foreign Aid Act of 1947 for France, Italy, and Austria.

CHAPTER 1

Europe Yesterday and Today

The failure of Europe to achieve economic recovery in the two and a half years following V-E Day[1] is not due primarily to the tactics of the Soviet Union. The Russians are simply taking advantage of a situation perfectly designed for their maneuvers. The real reasons for Europe's difficulties lie much deeper.

On the surface there is the devastation and exhaustion of the war. Great portions of London were laid in ruins; the Netherlands' dikes were pierced and much of the Dutch farm land was put out of commission; a broad belt of France from the coast to the German frontier was fought over; the same was true in Italy; the German economy lay prostrate and much of the Ruhr, the industrial heart of Europe, was in ruins. Added to all this, there had been a systematic destruction of the rail systems and their rolling stock.

Behind the immediate war destruction are the run-down mills, plants and mines, which were strained to the limit to provide armament and fuel, with little done for upkeep and repair. The plight of Europe in this respect was and is all but desperate. In many parts of Europe the farm land had been subjected to a similar strain with little done to keep up the fertility of the soil. This picture of physical destruction is bad enough, but almost easier to repair than the physical and moral damage wrought on millions of human beings. To peoples exhausted by years of war strain and occupation and spoliation by a cruel enemy and suffering from hunger and cold, the future seems to hold nothing but terror and despair. The population of Europe had been hopelessly jumbled up. Thousands of Jews and displaced persons were still in camps, awaiting some asylum somewhere. War prisoners by the thousands were working in the Allied countries, while the same impov-

1. Victory Europe Day, 8 May 1945, the date of the surrender of Germany.

5

erished Allies were pouring out money to maintain large armies. Germans were hustled out of Eastern Germany and Czechoslovakia so that the Poles and Czechs and Russians could move in. Train loads of Poles in the East who did not like the Russians had been carried off to work in Russian labor camps. Fifth columns, directed from Moscow, were building on want and despair to undermine existing social and governmental institutions. A single look at Europe was enough to make one ask with the psalmist: What is man, that Thou art mindful of him?

Large numbers of Europeans would already have starved long before the end of 1946 had it not been for the food and supplies largely furnished by the United States. And then came the coldest winter in many years, followed in 1947 by a summer of drought. Crops wasted away. The sum total of these depressing circumstances all but brought many of the West European nations to their knees.

That a healthy and prosperous Europe is essential if there is to be peace in the world can be demonstrated by historical precedent. That Europe will have to have some help from the United States can also be demonstrated. But there is no prospect that this help will effect recovery unless the Europeans can find some way to get together among themselves. It was the necessity of getting together that was the core of Secretary Marshall's speech. In effect, he was saying: The United States has given all the old-style help it can. The United States has lent or given money and goods to individual countries without any overall plan.[2] It is useless to do this any longer. The West European nations must figure out their common needs and common resources and reach some kind of common agreement as to what they are going to do about all these problems before the United States can give any practical assistance.

When, at the war's end in 1945, the peoples of Europe faced up to the task of making a new start, they were confronted not only with the devastation of war as I have described it above, but with major difficulties inherited from the distant past.

From the middle of the nineteenth century Western Europe had been rapidly transformed into an industrial society with an enormously increased population. It was a delicate and complicated mechanism. This West European society had made its living by

2. American aid to West European countries before that date had been in excess of $9 billion.

bringing to its mills raw materials from every quarter of the globe and selling them in similarly scattered worldwide markets. Its food came in part from intensively cultivated farm lands of its own, but more largely from Eastern Europe and from overseas.

To understand the present picture, it is worth while to consider how this all developed. In a sense, the trouble began in 1775 when James Watt and Matthew Boulton began the manufacture of steam engines at Birmingham.[3] Within twenty-three years, Eli Whitney, the inventor of the cotton gin, had worked out in his mind the ideas of mass production and the standardization of parts and had put these ideas into practice at a firearms factory in New Haven.[4] The engine and the machine process were turned loose in a world encrusted with feudal beliefs, where peasant agriculture and handicraft manufacture and merchant trading had been the rule for centuries.

In Britain great deposits of coal and iron lay close to one another. The combination of the engine, the coal and the iron brought the industrial revolution, in which England had a long running start. The effect of this revolution was to turn Britain into the workshop of the world. More than a hundred years ago Britain repealed the Corn Laws and become a free trading nation.[5] Her people were turned into industrial workers who subsisted on food brought in duty-free from abroad. Cotton from the American slave states was woven in Lancashire and sold throughout the world. Bessemer first made his steel in England and once the first railway proved a success in England, British rails and locomotives went abroad for the use of foreign railways.[6] The wooden shipping

3. The Scottish instrument maker Watt improved already existing steam engines. His inventions contributed substantially to the industrial revolution. Urged by his partner Boulton, Watt in 1781 invented a mechanism that allowed a rotating motion for the steam engine that before had been used mostly for pumping.

4. Best known for inventing the cotton gin, Whitney's major contribution to modern manufacturing process is believed to be the development of the concept of mass production of interchangeable parts. In 1801 Whitney supposedly displayed the result of this new system of mass production by assembling randomly selected parts of a rifle to one final product. Actually, Whitney did not invent the cotton gin, nor did he invent or even succeed in successfully applying the system of interchangeable parts. For the Whitney and many other legends, see Richard Shenkman, *Legends, Lies, and Cherished Myths of American History* (New York, 1989).

5. Corn Laws governed the British import and export of grain. After legislation protecting domestic grain production was instituted in 1791, the prices rose sharply. Bad harvests and the failure of the Irish potato crop in 1845, led to the repeal of all Corn Laws in 1846.

6. Sir Henry Bessemer developed the process of manufacturing steel inexpensively in 1856.

of other days was eventually displaced by the greatest fleet of merchant vessels ever known. In 1938 more than seven thousand British vessels of a hundred tons burden or more plied the oceans of the world.

The industrial age in continental Europe followed somewhat tardily in the wake of the French Revolution[7] and the Napoleonic wars.[8] But on the Continent industry did not have a free and unimpeded field as it did in the United States, nor did any Continental power have the sort of empire Britain had, though France and the Lowlands later developed outlets in Africa and the Far East. The Continent was a huge patchwork of independent states. There were kingdoms, grand duchies, papal states, free Hanseatic cities. Germany was littered with principalities ruled by princelings whose sole claim to position was divine right and whose grandfathers had sweated blood from the peasants to build miniature Versailles and to maintain miniature armies. As the nineteenth century wore on, Europeans of all nationalities moved out by the thousand in order to make a new start in America. A part of this territorial jigsaw puzzle was smoothed out when Bismarck consolidated the German states into the Empire in 1870[9] and when Italy was unified in the same year.[10]

In this clutter of independent nations the industrial development of the Continent got under way. The building of European railways had begun but a few years before and in middle Europe travellers could repeatedly enjoy the sensation of crossing an independent nation in less than half an hour.

Thus the economic foundations of modern Europe were laid. Since England was doing so well, the idea prevailed that free trade was a good thing and that the international gold standard was too.[11] With these fundamental arrangements accepted by all, sure-

7. The revolutionary movement in France culminated in the storming of the Bastille in Paris on 14 July 1789.

8. The Napoleonic wars, 1792 to 1815, were a series of wars with shifting French alliances, producing brief French hegemony of Europe.

9. Otto von Bismarck succeeded in uniting the numerous parts of Germany under the leadership of Prussia and thus founded the German Empire. He served as its first chancellor until 1890. After Prussia had won the Prussian-Austrian War in 1866 and the Franco-German War (1870–1871), the German Empire was finally created at Versailles, France, in 1871.

10. The final unification of Italy, in October 1870, was accomplished when French troops guarding the papal City of Rome left to take part in the Franco-German war. Italian troops occupied the city and broke the papal rule.

11. In a gold standard system, gold or a currency that is convertible into gold at a fixed value, is used for international payments. Full gold standard was in operation only from 1870 until 1914.

ly the world could look forward to uninterrupted peace and prosperity; or so they thought.

Families like the Rothschilds had banking houses scattered over Europe and money transactions were simple.[12] The international exhibition held in London in 185[1] at the Crystal Palace[13] began the era of world's fairs, attended by throngs of people who marveled at machine-made goods and the machines that did the making.

Coal, iron, steel, and railways made these things possible. Everything looked rosy. There was the British Empire with its shipping and its banking going to the ends of the earth. There was the United States, rugged, uncouth, and far away, tending to its own business, then caught up in a civil war and not then causing much concern to a sophisticated Europe. There was Russia, dark and vast and Asiatic, with an autocratic government ruling hordes of serfs who still used wooden plows in their primitive agriculture. And there was Western Europe, each nation developing its industry in its own way.

The British had had the good fortune to start off in the modern era with an empire, a sea-going tradition, a steam engine and great supplies of coal and iron. The Americans had had the good luck to start with an enormous country, plenty of resources and little interference. The Germans were less lucky, but they held some strong cards. They were not so talented in improvisation as the Americans and they were not, from direct experience, as world conscious as many of the British were, but they were strong on system and organization, the idea of professionally trained personnel was deeply rooted, and their reputation in many of the technical arts – lens making at Jena, for instance – was worldwide. Furthermore, the Germans had some natural resources of their own and the combination of technical skill and these resources now began to produce some remarkable results.

Some statistics at this juncture – 1900 – may be illuminating. In that year the United States, with an area of 3.6 million square miles, had a population of a little over 76 million. There was plenty of room for the Americans to move around in, which partly explains why the country has been able to almost double its popu-

---

12. The Rothschild family is the most famous of all European banking dynasties. Founded in the late eighteenth century, the German banking house with its headquarters in Frankfurt had established branches in London, Paris, Vienna, and Naples by 1820.

13. The Crystal Palace had been designed by Joseph Paxton and was later recognized as marking a revolution in style.

lation in the years since without blowing to pieces. The United Kingdom had an area of 120,979 square miles and a population of 41 million. That's a lot of people in a very small area, but there was the Empire as an escape hatch. Germany had an area of 208 thousand square miles and a population of 56 million. Italy and the Lowlands were beginning to feel the same problems of space and population. The increase in the population of Europe as a whole furnishes some startling figures. In the 150 years between 1650 and 1800, it increased only by an estimated 87 million. In the 140 years which followed it increased by over 320 million. Since 1750 Europe's population has nearly quadrupled.

Foreign sources of raw materials were being developed as populations to process them in Western Europe grew. Tariffs for the most part were low. Trade was free and travel was easy. In those good days an American who went abroad simply went down to the boat, bought his passage, and departed. He could have a passport if he insisted on it, but few Americans used them nor did the British either. They were thought to be of some value as identification if a person got entangled with a foreign police regulation, but in a pinch a letter, or almost anything, would serve as well, except in Russia, Turkey, and few other countries. Everybody's trade was growing, and at the turn of the century everything seemed to be going well. But there were danger signs.

Inside each of these nations an elaborately knit structure of industry, trade, and finance was growing up. The instinct to protect these structures was strong and pressures multiplied on every hand. The future life and health of a fast-growing population demanded that a series of European problems be faced and dealt with.

1. There was a growing difficulty in handling a complicated capitalism inside rigid national boundaries. Capitalism works through a never-ceasing swing of expansion and contraction. Bankruptcies are supposed to sweep out the economic weaklings and let the hardier specimens move on. In the end, every activity in life is a gamble, and the merit of capitalism was that when the gamble failed the failure swept a portion of the field clear for another try. Hard times affected the European nations variously, depending upon the state of development of their capitalist economies. Governments began experimenting with all sorts of devices to protect themselves against the vicissitudes of capitalism both at home and in neighboring nations.

2. Increasingly bitter competition among the European states in the outside world was a second factor. England, France, Germany,

Italy, Belgium, the Netherlands, and other countries came into sharp economic conflict in Africa and Asia and in a race for the oil resources of the Middle East. American export trade, backed by mass production methods at home, was also coming into the international market, as was that of Japan, as a disturbing factor to the somewhat more pedestrian methods of some of the European states.

3. The relics of a medieval caste system distorted the vision of large numbers of Europeans and repeatedly thwarted rational decisions. The Emperor Wilhelm[14] was able to speak of himself as being clad in shining armor; relations between Austria and Russia were strained when Count Ae[h]renthal, the Austrian ambassador, and Isvolski, the Russian foreign minister, began to pay attention to the same lady.[15] A sense of realism was strong enough in the various governments to prevent the Kaiser from trying to persuade the European crowned heads to support the King of Spain[16] in the Spanish-American War of 1898.[17] The whole struc-

14. Emperor Wilhelm II of Germany, known for his militaristic manner, reigned from 1888 until the end of World War I. In 1918 he was forced to abdicate.

15. Dulles is referring to the Bosnian crisis of 1908. Together with Herzegovina, Bosnia had been assigned by the Congress of Berlin (after the Russo-Turkish War of 1877–1878) to be occupied by Austria-Hungary, but remained officially a part of the Ottoman Empire. Developments in Turkey let Austrian foreign minister Alois von Aehrenthal to the conclusion that a new constitutional Turkish government might be formed, quite likely reclaiming Bosnia and gaining control over the region. Meeting with Russian foreign minister Aleksandr P. Izvolsky on 16 September 1908, Aehrenthal promised that his government would not object to the opening of the Bosporus and the Dardanelles to Russian warships (denied to Russia since 1841) in return for Izvolsky's agreement that Russia would not object to the annexation of Bosnia. When Austria-Hungary annexed Bosnia-Herzegovina on 7 October 1908, Izvolsky was unprepared and could not control strong popular opposition. Russia supported claims by Serbia that Austria cede a portion of that region to Serbia. Austria, in turn, was firmly supported by Germany, and threatened to invade Serbia. Russia had not been successful in mustering strong support from its ally France and could not risk war. In March 1909 Izvolsky notified Germany that Russia accepted the annexation. The resulting tensions between Serbia, Austria-Hungary, Germany, and Russia contributed to World War I. Differences in the spelling of the Russian foreign minister's last name occur because of differences in the transcription from the original cyrillic. In the notes, the current spelling is used.

16. Actually, in 1898 the King of Spain, Alfonso XIII, was not yet of age, and María Christina served as queen regent for her son until 17 May 1902. Her regency is commonly associated with tact and wisdom, giving Spain a measure of peace and political stability.

17. On the background of the Cuban struggle for independence and an (still unexplained) explosion sinking the U.S. battleship *Maine* in Havana Harbor, an armistice and Spanish plans for limited powers of self-government for Cuba did not satisfy the U.S. After the U.S. demanded the complete withdrawal of Spanish armed forces from Cuba, Spain declared war on the United States. The war was extremely one-sided in favor of the U.S. The whole of the Spanish fleet was sunk in

ture of society was antiquated, as the American founding fathers had realized a century before.

4. The burden of military establishments was growing. Professional armies disappeared at the end of the eighteenth century when the French Revolution brought in the idea of universal conscription. This, in turn, led to the idea of the nation in arms. At an increasingly rapid rate military budgets began to swell. The dead weight of these military establishments on European economies was in numerous instances crushing. Italy, for example, is a country with almost no natural resources besides water power. It survives on the industry of its people. From the moment of unification in 1870 the expansion of the military – and the navy! – began and never stopped. By 1914, Italy was up to its neck in armament debt.

5. The populations of many of the nations of Western Europe were growing faster than the opportunities afforded by the home economy. Somehow or other these populations had to be cared for. As early as the beginning of the nineteenth century, Malthus had become alarmed at this situation and predicted dire events if populations were not kept down.[18]Though his forebodings were premature, there may well have been more foresight in them than people are inclined to believe.

6. Europe was becoming a patchwork of watertight compartments. In each of these compartments an effort was made to build up a complete and self-sufficient economy. Each had to have every type of industry, even though there was not a broad enough market to expand the industry on an economic basis. Let us take a single example, that of motor cars. Practically every European country of any size had a considerable number of motor cars of its own national manufacture and yet a very limited clientele to which to sell them. Hence, they were custom-built affairs, so expensive as to be available only to the rich. As there was no mass consumption, there was no incentive for mass production.

By 1914, Europe was ready for a thorough overhauling, the par-

---

a matter of hours with only seven American sailors wounded. The war practically ended on 17 July, after the Spanish Caribbean fleet had been destroyed and the last Spanish stronghold at Santiago, Cuba, had surrendered. In the Treaty of Paris, signed on 10 December 1898, Spain waived all its claims to Cuba, ceded Guam and Puerto Rico to the U.S., and for $20 million sold the sovereignty over the Philippines to the United States.

18. British economist and demographer Thomas Robert Malthus is best known for his theory that growth of population will always exceed food supply. Only strict restrictions to reproduction, he claimed, would constitute a solution to the fate of mankind.

titions between the watertight compartments of sovereign states were increasingly subject to strain. Instead of having a house-cleaning and a get-together among the European states the Continent blew up in war.

Before trying to analyze what this meant to the European economy of today, it is worth while to see what had been happening in the British Empire, which was at one and the same time an integral part of Europe and an integral part of the outside world.

The building up of the British Empire was a long process, but the greater part of the job was accomplished in the century between Waterloo in 181[5] and the Battle of the Marne in 1914.[19] England, as the great manufacturing, industrial and financial center of the Empire, got raw materials from everywhere and sold the product everywhere. Since this was true, foreigners from all over the world went to London when they wanted to borrow money. In due course, the British [received] income from

1. The manufactured products she sold;

2. The freight charges paid for transport in British ships;

3. The insurance taken out in London on the cargoes;

4. Interest on money borrowed in London; and

5. Investments in foreign countries.

These transactions netted a large profit, much of which continued to be invested abroad. Such transactions also, in the course of time, had a revolutionary effect not only upon the British overseas dominions but upon independent nations as well.

Let us see how this worked. A typical illustration – only one of many which might be cited – is provided by the story of British relations with Argentina and the story of the Vestey family of Liverpool. Britain's transformation into a giant factory, with the consequent necessity of importing food, provided the Argentines with a ready-made market for their meat and grain and gave the

19. The Battle of Waterloo on 18 June 1815 brought about the final defeat of Napoleon by a combined British, Dutch, Belgian, and German force under the command of Arthur Duke of Wellington and Prussian forces commanded by Gebhard Leberecht Blücher, Fürst von Wahlstatt. The first Battle of the Marne was fought between 6 and 12 September 1914 during World War I. It was an offensive conducted by the French army and the British Expeditionary Force against advancing German troops who had invaded Belgium and France and were only thirty miles away from the Paris suburbs. The German army was forced back and had to dig in, thus preventing the anticipated swift and total victory against France. It was also the beginning of trench warfare.

13

British a reciprocal market for British goods. Gradually, British money began to be invested in Argentina – in ranches, hardwood lumbering operations, tannin extraction, and numerous other businesses. By 1880, Argentina had expanded economically to a point where a rail system would help it expand even faster. Into Argentina, therefore, poured the British money that built the Argentine railways. These roads, built by British engineers, laid with British rails and equipped with British locomotives and rolling stock, belonged almost wholly to British investors. Fanning out north, south, and west from Buenos Aires, the main purpose of the roads was to carry the meat and the grain down from the Argentine *estancias* to the British-owned elevators and packing plants at Buenos Aires.

Around this nucleus of interests others grew up. A British community in Argentina needed branches of British banks, British local newspapers, and British services of all kinds. Periodicals were crammed with the advertising of British firms and their columns, closely read in England, carried information which helped the British make their business decisions.

The great British Vestey interests had a humble start in Liverpool in the middle of the nineteenth century. The senior Vestey, a butcher, had a number of sons whose introduction to the meat business came from having to help the old man in his shop. These sons were an industrious and energetic group and presently set out to make their way in the world. At the time of the World's Fair of 1893 one of the Vestey sons had a large meat business in Chicago. All of them prospered and eventually, in combination, they controlled an enormous business. Having started as shopkeepers, they were retail minded and the result of their efforts was a great chain of retail stores scattered throughout the United Kingdom which were supplied with meat, fruit, and dairy products that came from Vestey sources all over the world.

The successful adaptation of refrigeration to ocean shipping was a powerful factor in the expansion of the Vestey interests, just as it was a powerful factor in world economics generally. It would be hard to measure what refrigeration meant to Australia. Australia raised wheat and wool, chiefly for the British market, but the amount of the wool grown was affected by problems of transportation. Shipment of livestock by boat was a wasteful and expensive process. But once refrigeration was perfected, Australian sheep raising boomed and the Vesteys, along with a lot of others, were on hand to put Australian mutton into Vestey-refrigerated ships and carry it to Europe.

Eventually, the Vestey interests became a huge complex of industries. They owned ranches in Australia, Brazil, and Argentina; they owned packing houses and refrigerator plants all over the world; they owned citrus groves. Their steamship lines sailed all the seas. Even the cotton wrappings for Vestey hams were woven in Vestey cotton mills. They sold their meat not only in Britain but all over the Continent.

An enterprise as vast as this employed a great many people, and the "hidden export" of British brains and talent found an outlet with the Vesteys. Young Englishmen went to the ends of the earth to work for the Vesteys, just as thousands of other Englishmen went to the ends of the earth to work for British enterprises in tin, rubber, diamonds, cocoa, copper, and scores of other industries.

This was the sort of empire that Rudyard Kipling[20] got excited about. Young Englishmen had before their eyes the example of men like Cecil Rhodes, who made a career, a fortune and – practically – an empire for himself in South Africa.[21] Rhodes disdained a title but plenty of others didn't. James Brooke, a few years earlier, had joined in the scramble in the East Indies and presently emerged as a ruling potentate, Raja Brooke of Sarawak,[22] with a kingdom all his own carved out of Borneo. Brooke in his life presented the interesting spectacle of an independent monarch subject to investigation by the House of Commons. When he died, his nephew succeeded to the title and dominions of the Brooke sultanate.

There was young Weetman Pearson, the engineer, who found Mexico to be a kind of Eldorado. He built the Tehuantepec railway there, he drained the Valley of Mexico, he built the port works of Vera Cruz, and then he poured the money into oil leases. He made

20. The English novelist and poet celebrated British imperialism. Kipling believed that every Englishman, and every other white man, had the obligation to bring culture and civilization to the heathen natives of not yet civilized areas. This has been described as "the white man's burden." In Kipling's view, everyone (with Americans and French only possibly exempted) born beyond the English channel was of a lesser breed.

21. The financier and statesman was the founder of British South Africa. From 1890 to 1896 he was prime minister of Cape Colony. Rhodes established the De Beers Consolidated Mines, Ltd., engaged in diamond mining.

22. After serving with the British East India Company and participating in the Anglo-Burmese war of 1825, Brooke fitted out an armed schooner and sailed to India in 1838. Arriving at Singapore, he learned that the chief minister of the sultanate of Brunei, Hassim, was at war with several tribes in Sarawank, a region under Brunei control. Brooke helped to crush the rebellion and as a reward was made Raja of Sarawank in 1841. The Brooke family ruled over Sarawank until 1 July 1946, when Sir Charles Vyner de Windt Brooke formally terminated Brooke rule.

so much money and made it possible for so many other Englishmen to make money that a grateful government raised him to the peerage as Lord Cowdray. And all the while the great Pearson engineering firm was taking on immense contracts all over the world. They even built the East River tunnels in New York City for the Pennsylvania Railroad.[23]

When Victoria held her Diamond Jubilee in London in 1897,[24] the Empire which she asked God to bless was shored up by just such persons as Pearson and the Vesteys, Rhodes, and Brooke. The beturbaned and bejewelled rajahs who attended the glittering festival were there by virtue of what not only Clive and Hastings[25] had done, but the efforts of thousands of British lieutenants, residents, engineers, traders, and speculators.

On the surface it seemed as though the Empire were unshakable – but under the surface a great revolution was taking place. The nature of that revolution was this: Britain exported not only goods for use but also machinery and process, as well as the know-how. It was certain to follow, as night the day, that the very countries which took machines and processes from Britain must presently begin to manufacture for themselves. Nor was this all. Other people began to improve on the British methods. The British, for example, were habituated to the use of natural dyes. The use of indigo, for instance, was natural enough, for long since the British had had colonies in which indigo could be grown. So it was in the use of dyewoods. But the Germans had no such traditions and no such tropical colonies. They did have chemists, however, and German chemists got the dyes out of bituminous coal from the Ruhr.

Similarly, the British were habituated to the apprentice system, the small enterprise and the large amount of handwork in manufacturing processes. Sheffield became a center of cutlery manufacture because there were deposits nearby of a high quality of abrasive stone, and there was a generous supply of water. Under these conditions, and with a seven-year apprentice system, Sheffield could make knives that would last for years. But when Americans

23. The British engineer went to Mexico in 1889. He first drilled for oil to acquire fuel for his locomotives. He controlled Mexican oil industry during the first two decades of the twentieth century. Elected to the British parliament in 1895, he was created Baron Cowdray in 1910 and viscount in 1917.

24. Queen Victoria reigned from 1837 to 1901.

25. Robert Clive was the first administrator of Bengal and was one of the chief creators of British rule in India. Francis Rawdon-Hastings was appointed governor general of Bengal and commander in chief of the forces in India in 1813. Hastings considerably strengthened British rule in India.

set about making cutlery they were neither aided nor hindered by the circumstances that were so helpful in Sheffield. The existence of a large domestic market looking for cheap cutlery resulted in the development of artificial abrasive and the mass production of inexpensive and serviceable knives. The proof of the American method was the production of a first-class kitchen peeler that sold for ten cents.

The final move was the rationalization of industry and the wholesale adoption of the idea of mass production. Rockefeller had shown what could be done with petroleum,[26] Swift and Armour did it with meat.[27] In 1900 came the organization of the United States Steel Corporation,[28] the first billion dollar corporation, and a giant the like of which had never been seen; then Ford, General Motors, and the great motor car industry. Every move in the United States seemed to expand the home market. It also sharpened the competition in the world market.

By the time World War I broke out,[29] the United States, with its efficient mass production methods, Germany, with its specialized industries, and Japan with cheap-labor goods, were beginning to cut into the monopoly of foreign trade which had been enjoyed by England, France, and the Lowlands. And at the same time, by evolution, the Empire was turning into a commonwealth, and the separate commonwealths had their own interests. The economic effects of both these developments were beginning to have repercussions in London, still the financial center of the world.

And England, though not integrally a part of the European continent and desirous as she might be to keep out of the quarrels of the Continent, was inexorably brought in. She was brought in at a time when, even if there had been no war, a readjustment of Britain's position in the world would have been inevitable.

26. John Davison Rockefeller realized the mercantile potential of the expanding oil industry, and, in 1870, founded Standard Oil Company which dominated the American oil industry until 1911 when the Supreme Court ruled it to be in violation of the Sherman Antitrust Act.

27. Gustavus Franklin Swift, a butcher's helper, invented the shipping of refrigerated meat from Chicago, "the nations slaughterhouse" to the East Coast in 1877. He successfully competed against rivals and established meat distributing houses and meat packing plants in the U.S. as well as in Southeast Asia. Philip Danforth Armour originated a number of new slaughtering techniques, use of waste products, and canned meat. Under his son, Jonathan Ogden Armour, Armour & Company became the largest meat-packing enterprise in the world.

28. The United States Steel Corporation, founded by scottish born Andrew Carnegie, was actually incorporated in 1901.

29. After declarations of war by Austria-Hungary against Serbia and by Germany against Russia, Germany first invaded Luxembourg and two days later, on 3 August, Belgium. The United States entered the war on 6 April 1917, after declaring war against Germany.

Even without two world wars, the Europe described above would no longer exist today. But the change might have come by an evolution one phase of which might well have included a great emigration from the overpopulated old world Continent. That movement was under way long before World War I and in the ten years before 1915 over ten millions of people emigrated from Europe to the United States alone – a rate of one million yearly. Other countries were then beginning to open their doors to emigration, and it is to these countries less heavily populated than the United States, in this hemisphere, in Africa and in Australia, that the bulk of the future emigration from Europe is likely to be directed.

At best, however, emigration is a slow process and can bring no real relief to Europe's problems for the next few years. In fact, if today large-scale emigration were permitted by the countries of Europe, in the present atmosphere of hopelessness which has gripped many of the youth of those countries, the best of the coming generations would be drained off – the men and women to whom Europe must look for the driving force to aid in recovery.

The task in taking up a program for European reconstruction is now vastly complicated by the fact that two wars have interrupted the logical evolution of events. They have prevented the readjustments of population by emigration, and they have abruptly cut Europe off from the external resources upon which it depended for the purchase of commodities essential to its economy. These resources might well have cushioned a peaceful change of its economy.

An effort was made between World War I and II to restore the old Europe, but it was a Europe gerrymandered by a rigid application of the rule of self-determination and characterized by extreme nationalism, untempered by economic good sense.

The principle of self-determination, high and noble in itself, has dangerous implications in the economic field. There is good reason to believe that Woodrow Wilson himself appreciated this. The Fourteen Points, the basis for the peace, did not advocate any broad principle of self-determination.[30] The people of Austria-Hungary and of Turkey were to be assured "autonomous" devel-

30. Declared by President Wilson on 8 January 1918 at a joint session of Congress, the Fourteen Points outlined his proposal for peace settlements after World War I. The relevant parts state that a free, open-minded, and absolute impartial adjustment of all colonial claims, should be made, based upon the strict observation that in determining all such questions of sovereignty the interest of the populations concerned must have equal weight with the equitable claims of the governments whose title is to be determined; and that the peoples of Austria-Hungary should be accorded the freest opportunity of autonomous development.

opment. It was only later, as nationalism got out of hand, that autonomy came to signify independence. And with this came the idea that all peoples everywhere should be entitled to transform themselves into nationally sovereign states despite the economic and the human wreckage that this principle carried with it in many parts of the world. Self-government implies self-restraint and must be imbedded in traditions of tolerance. When we start out to give this principle worldwide application overnight, we are subjecting the economy of the world to a grievous strain, as we found in the days between the two wars and as we find today.

In addition to the problems created by the application of this principle of self-determination high tariff walls were raised in the 1920's and, as economic conditions worsened, quotas and soft currencies added to the confusion. In the depression of the early 1930s we had on a small scale the beginning of the problems Europe is facing today.

The Europe that was driven into World War II by the insane ambitions of Hitler was already beginning to be a very different place from the Europe that entered World War I. The Europe that came out of World War II can never again be made into the pattern of pre-1914 days.

The reason is simple. Europe has lost a major part of the great overseas investments and resources of which at one time it had a monopoly. For example, it is estimated in a British White Paper published in 1945 that the United Kingdom's net capital position vis-à-vis the world has deteriorated by nearly $17 billion. Stated more simply, Britain is almost $17 billion poorer than she was. Europe, particularly Britain, has lost as well its exclusive position as carrier, insurance broker, and banker for the world. Europe can no longer afford the luxury of maintaining relatively small, compartmented economic units as it felt it could do before 1914 with the world to draw on. It will need to pool its resources, reduce its costs of production, develop a large measure of free trade within the European area, reduce its population by emigration, and redouble its efforts to develop in those areas of the world where it still has overseas and colonial possessions, particularly Africa, new sources of raw materials, commodities, and wherever possible, foodstuffs. The spirit of enterprise which built up the British Empire needs to be rekindled. There are still economic worlds open to peaceful conquest. Finally, Europe must strive to free itself from dependence on hard currency countries for its essential imports of food and raw materials until it can make its own money "hard" by balancing exports and imports.

19

International reforms will help. The stabilization of currencies, while it will not in itself provide enough food and cotton, fertilizer and agricultural equipment to meet the needs, will serve to bring out hidden assets and supplies of food which worthless currencies will not lure from the farmers.

But all this cannot be done overnight. The cure will require a considerable period of years, particularly the phase of it involving the development of new sources of wealth. Meanwhile Europe must have help, or she will starve physically and economically.

It was the full comprehension of this situation and the fact that Europe was reaching the end of its available economic resources which led Secretary Marshall to make his appeal to the countries of Europe to get together and, in effect, to tell the United States what Europe was prepared to do to help itself and what it considered were its essential needs from the United States so that the joint efforts of the European countries and of the United States would "assist in the return of normal economic health in the world, without which there can be no political stability and no assured peace."[31]

31. *FRUS, 1947*, 3: 237–39.

CHAPTER 2

Russia Turns Its Back on Europe

The significance of Marshall's speech was not grasped immediately in the United States. But London and Paris saw that it might well mark a milestone in the history of Europe. They reacted quickly, and there was a hurried exchange of diplomatic communication across the Channel.

One point of uncertainty, however, was particularly disturbing to the government in France. When Secretary Marshall spoke of Europe and Europeans, what did he mean? Did he intend to include or exclude Russia, which is both a European and an Asiatic power? If he did not include Russia in the invitation, there were elements of embarrassment for France and other countries. Acceptance might appear to be an overt act directed against Russia.

It is true that the speech made no direct reference to Russia. In fact, it did not refer to any individual country by name. The invitation was addressed to Europe, specifically to governments willing to assist in the task of recovery. To these governments it was a promise of cooperation. A clear statement was added, however, that "any government which maneuvers to block the recovery of other countries cannot expect help from us," nor could governments or groups "which seek to perpetuate human misery in order to profit therefrom politically or otherwise."[1]

The French hurriedly consulted Washington for clarification and on June 12 the secretary of state gave the answer. He had in mind the entire Continent west of Asia – the Soviet Union, or at least the European part of it, was most certainly included.[2]

Thus the way was cleared for the nations of Europe to act, and Ernest Bevin, the British foreign minister, flew to Paris on June 17

1. *FRUS, 1947*, 3: 237–39.
2. *New York Times*, 13 June 1947, 1.

to meet with his French colleague, Georges Bidault. They immediately dispatched an invitation to Molotov to join them and consider the manner in which Europe should respond to Secretary Marshall's proposal.

For once, it seemed that the Communist leaders did not have a ready answer. Marshall's speech had taken the initiative away from Russia and they were momentarily at a loss for effective counter measures. However, the invitation to meet with British and French ministers could hardly be ignored or abruptly dismissed. Molotov agreed to discuss the Marshall proposal and to do so in Paris. The date fixed by Moscow was June 27. Obviously, the Kremlin desired time for consideration and possibly to prepare counter measures. The Soviets had recently been tightening its grip in the satellite countries. The coup in Hungary had just taken place,[3] and shortly before Marshall made his proposal, the opposition leaders in Bulgaria and Yugoslavia, Petkov and Yovanovitch, were arrested.[4]

The first reaction of the Kremlin to Secretary Marshall's idea, as expressed by *Pravda*, had been hostile. The party line was already laid down. Ironically enough, it ran that the Soviet Union was determined to resist interference in the domestic affairs of small nations by the big powers.[5] In the House of Commons, Bevin warned the Soviet that the period of appeasement was over. He would not, he said, "be a party to holding up the economic recovery of Europe by the mess of procedure, terms of reference or all the paraphernalia that may go with it.... If there is to be a conflict of ideologies I shall regret it but if it is forced upon us we must face it."[6] Obviously, the British government was determined to go ahead, Russia or no Russia.

There is good reason to believe that the Soviet policy had not been finally determined, even as late as June 26, the date of Molotov's arrival in Paris with a staff of eighty-nine accompanying him. There were various straws in the wind to indicate this. The

3. Dulles is probably referring to the arrest of Béla Kovács in February 1947. Kovács, a member of the Hungarian parliament, had been accused of "counterrevolutionary" activity. When the Hungarian National Assembly refused to repeal his parliamentary immunity, he was arrested by the Soviets.

4. Nikola Dimitrov Petkov, leader of the Agrarian Party in Bulgaria, was executed on 23 August 1947 on charges of conspiring to overthrow the Fatherland Front government. The Yugoslavian politician Dragolub Yovanovitch was arrested on 17 May 1947 on charges of working for a foreign intelligence organization.

5. *Pravda* was the semiofficial newspaper of the Soviet Union. *New York Times*, 26 June 1947, 2.

6. *New York Times*, 20 June 1947, 1.

Polish government had tentatively indicated its intention of cooperating, followed by a somewhat feeble suggestion along the same lines from Yugoslavia. This could not well have happened if Moscow had already decided its course of action. Further, the French communists suddenly dropped their vigorous anti-American line, and Molotov's first statements at the conference left room for some hope. Several meetings were delayed while Molotov was trying to get the last word from Moscow.

It was a difficult and dangerous decision for the Soviet. On the one hand, there seemed to be here a great opportunity for Russia. As a participant in any plan for European reconstruction, she would certainly claim a substantial share of any credits or new lend-lease, or whatever form American aid might take. Some time earlier, Russia, through the back door, had suggested that she would like a billion dollar loan. The papers had been laid in some government department in Washington, as they had not gone through the usual channels. The request had been belatedly and politely answered, and thereafter there had been no further Russian reaction.[7]

But here the door to capital might be opening again, and even if Russia wished the European reconstruction plan to fail, would it not be better for it to fail because we refused or were unable to meet exorbitant Russian demands for money or for aid? There are a thousand ways by which Russia, if a participant in the plan, could have sabotaged it from within. Anyone knowing the temper of the American Congress, and we must assume that Russia knew it, could have predicted the difficulty, in the summer of 1947, of securing Congressional consideration for large new appropriations to aid Russia. And certainly the easiest way to prevent the

---

7. The United States had actually furnished more than $10 billion to the Soviet Union through Lend-Lease during World War II. The Lend-Lease Act became law on 11 March 1941, after in late 1940 it became clear that Great Britain and other powers fighting Germany were nearing the point of exhaustion of their dollar assets. It authorized the president to sell, exchange, transfer, lend, or lease war equipment and all other goods to any country he deemed necessary to the defense of the United States. Soviet Foreign Minister Molotov had requested a $6 billion loan for reconstruction under the generous Lend-Lease terms. The U.S. regarded Lend-Lease strictly as a war-time measure, and the loan was not granted. Lend-Lease shipments to the USSR, however, reached its height in May of 1945. In mid-May Lend- Lease to the Soviet Union was, abruptly and not very diplomatically, terminated. Settlement of the issue of repayment of Lend-Lease was stalled, when later that year Soviet officials indicated that the USSR regarded Lend-Lease as already compensated by the blood Soviet troops had shed in the fight against Germany and Japan.

passage of any European aid plan through Congress was to have a goodly percentage of such aid earmarked for the Soviet.

We will never know how these momentous issues were debated in the Kremlin. For they were momentous. Bevin is reliably reported as being convinced that this was a turning point in world history. Were the members of the Politburo all of one mind, or was the decision solely that of Stalin? It did not make much difference, since Stalin in 1929 had announced that all decisions in the Politburo were taken unanimously. For Russia the veto is an article of export trade only. A dictator does not need to disagree with himself. But it is a pity we do not know what trend the discussion in the Kremlin took before Stalin reached his unanimous decisions.

In writing of the policy formulated by Stalin in consultation with that small group of men called the Politburo, it is inevitable that one should fall into the habit of using the terms "Russia," "Soviet Union," "Communist Russia," and the like, almost interchangeably. It is well to remember, however, that as respects a particular decision taken by Moscow, it is difficult to state to what degree the action is motivated (1) by what we may call traditional Russian national and expansionist policy or (2) by the desire to promote a worldwide Communist revolution against the democratic nations in this two-world system which unfortunately exists today.

In any event, in referring to a policy formulated in the Kremlin, we are passing upon the acts of a dictatorship as absolute and as ruthless as any the world has ever seen, and when we speak of action taken by this dictatorship, we are neither condemning nor passing judgement on the millions of the Russian people who today have neither voice nor choice.

When, finally, the orders went out to Molotov to try to wreck the Marshall Plan even before it was born, a hard task was presented to even as wily a debater as he. He has had many strange theses to support, but never one as difficult to rationalize as this, and never in a debate was Molotov less coherent or persuasive than during the five days he was present at the Paris meeting.

At the outset of the conference there had been measured optimism. An official statement of the Soviet view was given by the Tass agency on June 29.[8] In general, it was not as unfriendly in tone toward the United States as usual, although it followed the Soviet line of suggesting that the United States was doing Europe a favor by taking this opportunity "for expanding its external mar-

8. TASS was the official news agency of the Soviet Union.

kets, especially in view of the approaching crisis." But here the Soviet thesis began to unfold. It was all very well for the European countries separately to tell their individual needs to the United States, but it will be an entirely different matter if the conference engages "in drawing up an all-embracing economic program for the European countries."[9]

Thereafter events moved rapidly to a climax, and on July 2 Molotov flatly and finally expressed the Soviet veto against collaboration in any collective plan for the revival of European economy. Such a plan, according to Molotov, would mean the loss by certain countries of their former economic and national independence at the dictates of other and stronger powers. Poland against its will might have to produce more coal at the expense of other branches of Polish industry, or Czechoslovakia might be forced to increase her agriculture and reduce her engineering industry at the wishes of other powers. Norway might be compelled to discontinue her steel industry because that was convenient for certain foreign steel corporations. Small states would lose their independence. The Anglo-French plan for setting up an Economic Coordinating Committee was rejected "as being altogether unsatisfactory and incapable of yielding any positive results."[10]

It would lead, said Molotov, "to Great Britain, France, and that group of countries which follows them separating themselves from the other European states and thus dividing Europe into two groups of states and creating new difficulties in relations between them."[11] Thus Russia, it seems, was trying to make England and France and the United States the parents of the Iron Curtain. It was we, not Russia, who were dividing Europe.

Obviously, it was the Russian plan that each nation must go on its own and starve in its own way. Any common plan for economic collaboration was viewed by the Soviet as vicious and dangerous. In threatening language the Soviet foreign minister said that he "considere[d]" it necessary "to caution the governments of Great Britain and of France against the consequences" of the proposed action as having "nothing in common with the real interests of the peoples of Europe." *Divide et impera* was the underlying Soviet theme. The West European countries must be just as "independent" as Poland, Rumania, Bulgaria, and the other satellites.[12]

9. *New York Times*, 30 June 1947, 4.
10. For the text of Molotov's statement and excerpts from Bevin's and Bidault's responses, see *New York Times*, 3 July 1947, 4.
11. Ibid.
12. Ibid.

Bevin was clearly outraged. "Mr. Molotov's objections to the Franco-British program," he stated, "were based on a complete travesty of the facts and a complete misrepresentation of everything the British Government had submitted. I suppose the method is to go on repeating these misrepresentations in the hope that someone would at last believe them."[13]

Noninterference in the internal affairs of other countries and respect for the sovereignty of other powers were declared by Bevin to constitute a fundamental principle of British policy.

> Britain will continue to strive for the unity of Europe, for the independence of Europe and for the independence of its national units. I regret that Mr. Molotov has threatened that if we continued this beneficent work we must face grave consequences.
>
> Well, my country has faced grave consequences and threats before. It is not the sort of prospect which will deter us from doing what we consider our duty.[14]

Bevin's remarks were so pithy and direct that when the careful French Foreign Office reproduced the documents of the conference it gave Molotov in full but omitted Bevin's speech entirely though it had already appeared in the daily press. But it did reproduce the equally candid and courageous answer of Bidault. Referring to Molotov's parting threat about the division of Europe into two camps, he remarked that this put his country on guard then he added, "I would like for my part to put the Soviet delegation on guard against any action which might result in separating Europe into two groups." Rejecting the thesis that France and Britain were trying to dominate smaller states or to impose their economic or political will upon them, he concluded his statement with these words: "Independence is not achieved in misery and isolation but affirmed in human cooperation and prosperity."[15]

I have devoted considerable space to this meeting in which Russia turned her back on Europe because it is a decisive point in European history. It marked the cleavage in Europe which up to this point western statesmen had been loath to acknowledge. Russia, in effect, said to the countries of Western Europe – "you must remain separate, unconnected, uncooperative states so that we can deal with you one at a time; you must not unite for your common economic betterment or for your common good; if you do unite we will consider that *you* are dividing Europe into two parts."

13. Ibid.
14. Ibid.
15. Ibid.

To emphasize the abruptness of his warning, Molotov gathered around him his large staff of eighty-nine secretaries, interpreters, and guards and made for the airport in the dead of the night, eschewing the usual diplomatic farewells. At 4:00 A.M. on July 3 his plane left Paris for Moscow.

Possibly there were other reasons for his hurry. He must have known that he had failed to check the determination of England and France to proceed with their plan for making a collective European reply to the Marshall invitation. How many of the European states would join in the common action was then unknown. But Soviet diplomacy had only a few days in which to work in order to keep that number as low as possible.

On July 3, when Molotov had hardly reached Moscow, an invitation went out from Paris to twenty-two European nations. They were asked to join in a conference in Paris on July 12. "Europe must begin by helping herself and by developing her basic production." This, plus assistance from the United States, which would play a decisive part, would be the best way to insure economic recovery, the invitation said.[16]

The task before the European committee was outlined in the invitation. Six subcommittees to deal with (1) food supplies, agriculture, (2) power, (3) transport, (4) raw materials, (5) equipment, and (6) iron and steel were proposed. To indicate that the United Nations organization was not to be by-passed, it was stated that the U.N. and its various technical organizations would be consulted.[17]

Today there are twenty-seven separate sovereign states in Europe, counting Russia as only one state rather than the three which have votes in the United Nations. All were invited to the Paris conference, except Spain, "provisionally" excepted because of the Franco government, and Germany, because it had no government.[18] Russia had already refused, and, subtracting the two inviting powers from the remaining twenty-four, we get the total of twenty-two to which formal invitations were sent. Of the twenty-two, sixteen accepted, having an estimated aggregate population today of some 270 million people if one includes Western

16. The English-language text of the British-French communique on the European reconstruction program, dated 3 July 1947, is reprinted in *New York Times*, 4 July 1947, 2.

17. Ibid.

18. Spain was ruled by Fascists under the leadership of Francisco Franco. Spain had been neutral during World War II but had aided Germany against the Soviet Union. After World War II Spain was, for some time, isolated politically.

Germany and the Saar with an estimated population of 49.8 million. Nine nations declined, having a population of 280 million, not including Eastern Germany. Of these 280 million, over 190 million are in the Soviet Union. Strikingly enough, the population of Europe west of the Iron Curtain, if one includes Spain, and the population of Eastern Europe, including Eastern Germany but deducting the peoples east of the Urals, come very close to balancing, each being between 250 million and 300 million. The lineup of the participating and nonparticipating countries, with their populations and areas is given below.

The hours which Molotov gained by his abrupt departure from Paris were badly needed to keep the Russian bloc in line. The Tass [a]gency quickly reported that Poland, Yugoslavia, and Rumania would refuse the invitation, but all three at first repudiat-

Nations Participating in Marshall Program*
(Not including Germany)

	SQUARE MILES	POPULATION
Austria	32,369	7,055,000
Belgium	11,775	8,400,000
Denmark	16,575	4,330,000
France	212,741	41,100,000
Greece	50,267	7,700,000
Iceland	39,709	130,000
Eire	26,601	2,955,000
Italy	119,733	46,000,000
Luxembourg	999	300,000
Netherlands	12,742	9,530,000
Norway	124,556	3,065,000
Portugal	35,424	8,275,000
Sweden	173,341	6,750,000
Switzerland	15,940	4,485,000
Turkey	296,500	19,100,000
United Kingdom	93,991	49,700,000
Totals:	**1,263,263**	**218,875,000****

* *New York Times*, 13 July 1947, sec. IV, 1.

** The CEEC Report's estimate is 219,300,000 [Dulles is referring to the Committee of European Economic Co-operation report, dated 21 September 1947, reprinted in U.S. Department of State, Office of Public Affairs, *Committee of European Co-operation: Volume I, General Report, Paris, September 21, 1947* (Washington, D.C., 1947; Department of State Publication 2930, European Series 28)].

Non-Participating Nations[19]

	SQUARE MILES	POPULATION
Albania	10,631	1,140,000
Bulgaria	42,741	7,000,000
Czechoslovakia	49,321	12,300,000
Finland	130,160	3,870,000
Hungary	35,911	8,900,000
Poland	120,782	22,600,000
Rumania	91,934	15,900,000
Yugoslavia	95,983	15,700,000
Russia	8,308,634	193,000,000
(including Asiatic areas)		
Totals:	**8,886,097**	**280,410,000**

ed the statement. Czechoslovakia was to be represented at the conference by her ambassador in Paris.

But Soviet diplomacy moved swiftly and firmly. Poland reversed itself and with Rumania sent refusals. Hungary, Yugoslavia, Bulgaria, and Albania followed suit. Finland was forced to say no. The minister president of Thuringia in the Russian zone of Germany, Rudolf Paul, who had repeatedly endorsed the Marshall Plan both orally and in writing, was shocked to read over his signature in the local press a denunciatory blast against the Plan which he had never seen before. He took the hint and fled over the border into Bavaria.[20]

Czechoslovakia was still troublesome. This country had declared its intention of attending the Paris conference and had even consulted with Poland on the subject when the Marshall program was first announced at which time the two countries had been in agreement that they should accept. Finally, however, Czechoslovakia's Communist prime minister, Klement Gottwald, and its foreign minister, Jan Masaryk, flew to Moscow and quickly

19. *New York Times*, 13 July 1947, sec. IV, 1.
20. *New York Times*, 28 December 1947, 7. Rudolf Paul had left the Soviet zone already on 1 September 1947 and had lived near Wiesbaden, Hessia, until he went to Munich, Bavaria, on 25 December. Another and probably more likely reason for Paul's flight from Thuringia could have been that information about his activities during the Third Reich were surfacing. Paul had been an early member of the Nazi Party and had divorced his Jewish wife, as he had admitted, to save his considerable wealth. See also *New York Times*, 6 September 1947, 6.

withdrew their tentative acceptance. That made the Soviet lineup complete.[21]

It was an uneasy victory, and it showed Moscow what germs of danger lay in the Marshall Plan. In the case of Czechoslovakia, the Soviet found it wise to temper their pressure with the promise of substantial deliveries, 200 thousand tons of grain, a promise that was later doubled.

The experience with their worried satellites and the, to Moscow, unexpected vigor shown by the West European countries in proceeding to work together to realize a Marshall Plan in defiance of the Molotov threats, persuaded the Soviet that vigorous countermeasures were necessary. Trade agreements were hastily entered into with a number of the satellite states. I have already mentioned the trade pact between Russia and Czechoslovakia, which Premier Gottwald brought back from Moscow in partial payment for refusal to cooperate in the Marshall Plan. On July 12, Bulgaria completed an $87 million trade agreement with Russia for 1947–1948. Five days later a trade pact was signed between Russia and Hungary and, on July 18, with Finland. Even little Albania received, on July 27, a promise of some machinery. Finally, on July 29, the Soviet government concluded an agreement with Yugoslavia. In general, these were all barter arrangements and the dollar sign merely evidences the value of goods to be delivered by each side. In this type of agreement Communist negotiators find the capitalist dollar the best standard of real value.

Thus the pattern of the Molotov Plan developed. Separate promises, separately arrived at. Russia was obviously worried at the extent to which her satellites were trading with the West and the outcome of these agreements was to tighten Russian control over the exports of the satellites and to divert their products eastward.

But the policy had another facet. As Senator Vandenberg[22] put it in his speech of November 25, 1947, "the wrecking crews" were "turned loose."[23] The instrumentality for this was a revived Communist international organization, this time labelled the

21. Actually, Gottwald instructed his administration in Czechoslovakia by telephone from Moscow to announce the withdrawal on 10 July. See *New York Times*, 11 July 1947, 1; and *New York Times*, 13 July 1947, 1.

22. Senator Arthur H. Vandenberg was the influential chairman of the Senate Foreign Relations Committee.

23. For the text of Vandenberg's speech, see *New York Times*, 25 November 1947, 14.

Cominform to distinguish it from the uneasily interred Comintern.[24] The Cominform embraced the Communists of nine nations, Russia, Yugoslavia, France, Italy, Poland, Bulgaria, Czechoslovakia, Hungary, and Rumania. Its target was the Marshall Plan and "Anglo-American imperialism." To emphasize the part of the satellites in the new organization, it was set up at conferences held in Warsaw early in October 1947. Its headquarters were to be located in Belgrade.

In its manifesto, released in Warsaw on October 5, the Cominform stated, "The Truman-Marshall plan is only a farce, a European branch of the general world plan of political expansion being realized by the United States of America in all parts of the world." We – that is, we Americans – according to the Cominform were planning the economic and political subjugation of Europe and then of China, Indonesia, and South America. "The aggressors of yesterday – the capitalist tycoons Germany and Japan – are being prepared by the United States of American for a new role – as tools for the imperialistic policy in Europe and Asia of the United States of America."[25]

General Andrei A. Zhdanov, a member of the Politburo and secretary of the Communist party's Central Committee, who was the Russian representative at the organization meeting of the Cominform, felt called upon really to dot the i's and cross the t's. In a declaration published in Moscow on October 22, he declared war on the Marshall Plan, which, he said, was designed to create an "American protectorate in which European countries were predestined to become the forty-ninth state." Then he added, "The U.S.S.R. will put all effort in seeing that the Marshall Plan is not realized."[26]

Acting Secretary of State Robert A. Lovett, in commenting on the organization of the Cominform, remarked that it would carry "to new lengths the distortions of United States policy." The Soviet, he said, "have made clear their intention to prevent, if they can, the economic recovery of Europe."[27]

Mr. Lovett's predictions have certainly been borne out. The lat-

24. The Comintern, also called the Third International, had been founded in 1919 to promote world revolution and functioned foremost as a agency of Soviet control over Communist movements.

25. *New York Times*, 6 October 1947, 3.

26. *New York Times*, 23 October 1947, 3. Alaska and Hawaii not yet been admitted to the United States of America.

27 *New York Times*, 9 October 1947, 1. For the full text of Lovett's comment, see ibid., 16.

est line of attack is that the Marshall Plan is a disguised program "to transform Western Germany into an arsenal of American expansion." The bulk of the money under the Marshall Plan goes to Germany, the Moscow Radio announced on December 22, 1947. "When the United States announces a four-year program of expenditure to revive Germany's heavy industry, her war potential, one recalls another four-year program for the development of German economy: The notorious plan of Goering and Hitler." This plan was adopted in 1936 and masterminded by Schacht,[28] and Moscow implies that the same sinister figure is behind the Marshall Plan. "The essence of the two plans is the same – war."[29]

While the Moscow propaganda machine continued to grind out its attacks on the Marshall Plan, the Soviet board of strategy had to face some rather disturbing problems. They had probably counted on their ability to keep the satellites in line, but the Communist parties in countries like France and Italy were in a more difficult position. What would happen to Maurice Thorez in France[30] and Palmiro Togliatti in Italy[31] if the order went out from Moscow that they, too, must oppose the Plan which meant food for the hungry and coal for the frozen populations of France and Italy? To ask the French and Italian Communists to stand up and be counted on this issue should have given Moscow real concern.

The Communist parties in these countries had often found difficulty in reconciling the Moscow line with the nationalist line. For them to take an out-and-out antinationalist line spelled disaster locally. The embarrassment of the Communists in Italy over the Trieste issue is an example.[32] With the advent of the Marshall Plan, the Communist parties in Western Europe were faced with a

30. Hjalmar Schacht had been minister of economics from 1934 to 1937. The Four-Year Plan had been adopted to fight unemployment in Germany and, at the same time, to make rearmament possible.

31. *New York Times*, 9 October 1947, 1, 16.

32. Thorez, leader of the Communist party of France, who had been associated with the Comintern, was a member of the French Chamber of Deputies from 1946 to 1958. He served as a deputy premier in 1947.

33. Togliatti, a former member of the secretariat of the Comintern, was leader of the Communist party of Italy.

34. The Italian city of Trieste, seized by Germany in 1943 as a southern port for the Third Reich, was occupied by Yugoslav troops under Marshall Tito in 1945 and was claimed for Yugoslavia. The Paris Peace Treaty of 10 February 1947 created the Free Territory of Trieste and provided for United Nations guarantees. The territory was administered jointly by a America-British administration and by Yugoslavia. The Free Territory status led to frictions between Italy and Yugoslavia and to frictions between the Communist parties of the two countries.

new dilemma: whether to follow the Cominform or to follow the line of national interest and support the Marshall Plan on which economic recovery depended. Under the surface, this issue seems to have driven a wedge into Communism. This was indicated by the disastrous failure of the December strikes in France and Italy, which, in turn, reflected the unpopularity which the Communist parties in these countries had brought upon themselves by their failure to back the Marshall Plan. It was also indicated by the split in the French labor movement, the CGT,[33] between the Communist and the anti-Communist wings. It is far too early to say that the Communist power in countries like France and Italy has been broken, but the Marshall Plan has dealt it a body blow from which it is staggering. Nenni, leader of the Italian left-wing socialists allied with the Communists,[34] has been forced by his followers to go so far as to express gratitude for American aid. And not only has the prospect of a Marshall Plan thrown dissension into the ranks of the extreme left wing and Communists, it has everywhere heartened the friends of liberty and democracy and the middle-of-the-road parties throughout Europe. It has been responsible in no small measure for giving these parties renewed strength to put up a fight against communism.

The reverses suffered by the extreme left-wing and Communist fronts in Western Europe are not likely to change the general course of Soviet policy regarding the Marshall Plan. They have announced their policy clearly and could not change it without loss of face. They have stated that they will do their best to wreck the Plan and they will continue on this course and will not be deterred by what they believe are temporary reverses here and there.

What they have not told us are the real reasons underlying their attitude. Why is it that Russia refused to play along with the Marshall Plan, even if she wished to see it fail and even though she realized, as well she might, that her participation in it would be the one element most likely to make it fail?

It is not easy to answer this question with any assurance. But it is worth while to try to find some answer, because the answer might help to furnish a key to Russian conduct for the immediate future.

A subtle – possibly oversubtle – suggestion is that Russia is so confident of defeating the Marshall Plan that she deliberately embarked on a policy which would be most likely to impel us to

33. Confédération Général du Travail.
34. Pietro Nenni had stated on 28 December 1947 that "Italy can neither give her adhesion to the Marshall Plan unconditionally nor reject it in its entirety." See *New York Times*, 29 December 1947, 6.

continue with it. Or, to put it another way, Russia wants to see us expend our hopes and our treasure on Western Europe, confident that she can wreck the West European economy anyhow and that she could then force the United States to withdraw, weak and disillusioned, to the Western Hemisphere.

The correct answer is probably simpler than this. Russia does not dare open her doors to [W]estern influence to the extent that cooperation in the Marshall Plan implies. Further, she does not wish to risk the effect of the Marshall Plan upon satellites who, in the two and a half years since V-E Day,[35] have on occasion shown far more interest in trade with the West than is pleasing to Moscow.

Trade is no easy thing to control, particularly by artificial bonds. You can buy a measure of economic allegiance by deliveries of foodstuffs in time of need, but it would be difficult and risky for Russia to attempt to shut off trade between Eastern and Western Europe entirely. At the same time, Russia knows that to let this trade continue is also a danger to her. If Poland, Rumania, and Czechoslovakia – to take three of Russia's neighbors which have the greatest economic potential and which are also the three countries having the closest ties with Western Europe – should allow their economies to be linked with the West, this might well, in time, undermine the Communist forces which control the first two of these countries and which head up the government in Czechoslovakia.

Russia, from her viewpoint, already had good cause for alarm in watching the recent development in the trade relations of countries like Poland and Czechoslovakia. In the first half year of 1947 Russia received less than 40 percent of all Polish exports, or about one-half of what the Soviet Union had received in the previous year. Most of the balance went westward. Poland, by sending a good part of its exportable surplus of coal westward, particularly to such countries as Sweden and Switzerland, has been able to secure vitally needed machinery and other products. Poland has also a potential exportable surplus of grain, which likewise could be exchanged almost anywhere in Europe for the capital goods she needs. Under a Marshall Plan it is easy to see that in a short time Poland might well develop a dependency on western markets, and she could have supplied to those western markets coal and grain which they vitally need today.

Russia sees the dangers in such a trade relationship. It is danger-

35. Victory Europe Day, 8 May 1945.

ous not only because it might help to make the Marshall Plan work, but because of the seeds of democracy, or, as the Russians would put it, of capitalist poison, which might follow the lines of trade.

The economic position of Czechoslovakia is very similar to that of Poland. Normally, Russia figures to only a minor degree in the trade of Czechoslovakia. Except for the trade with her immediate neighbors, her major trade relations are with the West. Now, under the principles laid down in the "Molotov Plan" trade agreement signed December 11, Russia's share in Czechoslovakia's total world trade is to be increased more than threefold, but even this would raise it from only 5 percent to approximately 16 percent. According to this trade agreement, which is to last for five years, the two countries are to exchange $100 million worth of goods each year. The Czechs are to export to Russia rails, locomotives, railway equipment, machinery, shoes, agricultural products, textiles, glassware, and crockery, while Russia is to send Czechoslovakia grain, raw materials, fertilizer, and chemicals, including, according to Russian promises, 400 thousand tons of grain and 200 thousand tons of fodder in 1948.[36]

The pattern of the agreement is interesting as setting the lines of the Molotov Plan. It is a barter agreement; goods are to be exchanged, valued and then a balance struck.

Czechoslovakia is truly in a difficult position. It is a neighbor of Russia and it is crowded up against two of Russia's satellites, Poland and Hungary. We cannot expect it to ignore Russian pressure to increase its trade relations with the East. But this little country treasures its political and economic independence, and it proposes to continue to trade with the West. Hubert Ri[p]ka, the Czechoslovak minister of foreign trade, made a very frank statement about the Marshall Plan and pointed to the contribution which Czechoslovakia was making "to the economic convalescence of Europe." "Our efforts," he said, "in no way run counter to the basic principles of Secretary of State Marshall's policy as directed toward the prosperity of all Europe." And he added

> The Marshall Plan will directly increase the import and export trading possibilities of all states taking part and will thus indirectly increase their possibilities of trading with states that are not taking a direct part in the plan. Every improvement of the economic situation in any part of Europe will certainly contribute indirectly to the prosperity of the rest of Europe.[37]

36. New York *Herald Tribune*, 12 December 1947, 1, 18.
37. *New York Times*, 4 January 1948, 5. The block quotation actually precedes the other quotes in Ripka's statement.

What the Czech minister of trade has said is undoubtedly what the corresponding ministers in Poland and Rumania would like to say if they had the freedom to do so. Russia realizes all this and sees in it a potential danger. In considering the Marshall Plan, the Soviet leaders probably adopted a line of reasoning somewhat as follows: If we, the Soviet agree to cooperate with the Marshall Plan, *a fortiori* all our satellite states, having an economy which usefully supplements that of Western Europe, will be tied in with West European economy and are likely to fall politically and ideologically under the influence of the West. As we, the Soviet, no longer have sufficient military forces in these countries to exercise absolute control over their destinies, and as it is essential to our safety to control them, we must do so by forging the strongest economic ties between them and the East; we must try to cut the ties between the satellite states and the West.

This is the essence of the Molotov Plan. In the eyes of the Russians it has a dual political and economic purpose. Economically, it renders the realization of the Marshall Plan far more difficult than it otherwise would be. Politically, it strengthens the ties that bind the satellites into the Communist orbit.

Certainly it is no part of the Marshall Plan to help build up a Molotov Plan by encouraging a trade embargo between Eastern and Western Europe or by cutting off trade between the United States and Czechoslovakia or the satellite countries. Quite the contrary. The administration's attitude, as indicated in the executive report,*** is as follows:

> The objective of the program, and of United States assistance toward European economic recovery, will be well served by a maximum of healthy trade relations internally within the Continent of Europe. Further, despite the fact that certain eastern European countries are presently prevented from participation in the European recovery program, no constraint should be extended by the United States to prevent their cooperation in achieving the objectives of that program. These objectives are fully consistent with those of the United Nations and its affiliated Economic Commission for Europe, an agency in which both eastern and western European nations meet to work for the common economic welfare of Europe.
>
> While the United States will provide no direct assistance under the program to nonparticipating European countries, it should interpose no obstacle to the exchange with such countries of the products which western Europe is in a position to supply for the commodities and materials needed by western Europe and which will materially assist in

*** See page 41.

the success of the program. This should hold true even through [sic] the products delivered by western Europe result in some minor degree from the processing of materials supplied by the United States or as a result of United States assistance to European recovery. The reexport of American goods substantially in the form in which they are received should not be permitted.[38]

When Molotov's threats in Paris failed to sway the West European powers in their determination to accept Secretary Marshall's challenge to Europe to unite, the Soviet not only evolved its own plan to bring the satellites into the Russian economic sphere, but it also directed all the intricate technique of a police state to the task of sabotaging the Marshall Plan and preventing, if it could, the economic recovery of Europe.

It is well to be realistic about the reasons for Russia's desire to see European reconstruction fail. Three times, if we go back to the Napoleonic era, Russia has been invaded from Western Europe. Russian memories are long, and they put much more weight on what they have learned from history than on any protestations of friendship or peaceful intentions which they hear at the present time. They propose that Western Europe shall be so weakened and so dominated by them that they shall never hereafter be in danger from the West. They believe that Western Europe, divided into many watertight, compartmented sovereignties and cut off from its natural markets in the East, can slowly be reduced to a position of impotence. While they have at times professed the belief that a Communist system can exist side by side with a system of free men, certainly they do not want an economically vigorous and healthy Western Europe so near the Iron Curtain. They don't like the comparison. Hence, they have declared their unalterable opposition to a united Europe.

The pattern of Russian policy following 1939 is clear. At that time Russia encouraged Germany to turn westward, in the hope that a long drawn-out conflict between Germany and the Western powers would bleed the [W]est and leave Russia dominant in Europe.

Molotov in his statement on Soviet foreign policy at the Extraordinary Fifth Session of the Supreme Soviet of the USSR on October 31, 1939, a speech made just as Russia consolidated its partnership with Germany over the stricken body of the Polish

---

38. U.S. Department of State, *Outline of European Recovery Program* (Washington, D.C., 1948; printed for the use of the Senate Foreign Relations Committee) 51–52.

state, put the story clearly. Soviet- German relations, he then said, were based on a "firm foundation of mutual interest....We have always been of the opinion that a strong Germany is an indispensable condition for a durable peace in Europe....We have consistently striven to improve our relations with Germany and have wholeheartedly welcomed similar strivings in Germany herself."

Germany's quick victory on the Continent crossed up the Soviet plans and left her in grave jeopardy. But our common victory over Germany, followed by some wishful thinking on our part as to Russian policy at Teheran, Yalta, and Potsdam,[39] have now left Stalin in a position where at long last he sees the possibility of achieving Russia's historical objective of absolute supremacy in Europe. Moscow proposes to work toward it by economic strangulation and by fomenting internal discord, probably not by military aggression. The Iron Curtain will be pushed forward as opportunity permits.

The Soviet Union has entered on a great gamble. In its challenge to the democratic forces in the world it is counting not so much on the strength of its own system, as on failure of ours. This challenge can only be met effectively if this fact is clearly understood by the free peoples of the world.

39. The meeting at Teheran, 28 November to 1 December 1943, marked the first meeting of the heads of states of the Big Three (Roosevelt, Churchill, and Stalin). Tentative plans were made for the establishment of an international organization for peace. At the meeting at Yalta, 4 February to 11 February 1945, the heads of state agreed that the liberated countries in Europe should have representative governments chosen by free election. The Soviet Union pledged to enter the war effort against Japan and gave a definite assurance that it would participate in the founding of the United Nations. At Potsdam, 17 July to 2 August 1945 (with Harry S. Truman, who had succeeded Roosevelt after his death, representing the United States; Churchill until 29 July, when he was succeeded by Clement Atlee, after Labour won the elections in Great Britain for the United Kingdom; and Stalin representing the Soviet Union), agreement was reached that Germany should be divided in four zones of occupation but should be treated as an economic unit.

CHAPTER 3

The Meeting of the Sixteen

The Paris conference met despite the Soviet withdrawal. For once the Russian veto did not stop the proceedings. The delegates of sixteen European nations representing, with Western Germany, some 270 million people, or approximately twice the population of the United States, gathered together in Paris on July 12, 1947. Their purpose was to draw up a program for European recovery in answer to Secretary Marshall's invitation.

This meeting – its official name was Committee of European Economic Cooperation (CEEC) – was significant in more ways than one. It was the first important postwar international conference at which Allies, neutrals, and former enemies sat down together to discuss a common problem, and they met together on a footing of equality. The Allies present were Belgium, Denmark, France, Greece, Luxembourg, the Netherlands, Norway, and the United Kingdom. All but the last of these had suffered German occupation. Of the neutrals, there were Eire, Portugal, Sweden, Switzerland, and Turkey. Italy and Austria were the former enemies, but both, in a sense, had been for a time enemy-occupied countries.[1] I hardly know where to class the sixteenth and smallest, Iceland – formerly a part of Denmark and now an independent nation.

In a sense, they were discussing the liquidation of the war in the economic field. But it was really more than that. It might well mark the beginning of an effort which could bring a step nearer the establishment of a United States of Europe.

On September 22, two months and ten days after their first meeting, the CEEC concluded and signed its report. It was unani-

---

1. Austria had been made part of Germany in 1938. Italy had fought under Mussolini on Germany's side. After Mussolini was ousted from power, Italy was in effect partially occupied by German troops under SS-General Karl Wolff.

mous, without reservation, equivocation, or destructive qualifying footnote. It went forward to Washington to Secretary Marshall in response to his request for a statement by the European countries as to the part they could play "to give proper effect to whatever action might be undertaken by this Government."[2]

The CEEC report in many ways is a remarkable document, not only for the candor with which the sixteen stated the problems facing Europe, but also for their directness in stating what they proposed to do about it. Of course, one can say that it is not very difficult to draw up a list of what one would like to receive. But it is not too easy to agree on the limitations to be set on those requests. Nor was it always a simple matter for the sixteen countries to agree on the concrete measures they themselves proposed to take.

The work of the conference had begun by seeking from each of the participants a statement of their needs over the coming four years. These estimates, added up and translated into dollar figures, reached somewhat alarming proportions. When the total, some $29 billion, seeped out to the press and reached the ears of the American government, the under secretary of state, Will Clayton, who had been guiding the American delegation at the intricate tariff negotiations at Geneva,[3] proceeded to Paris and sat down with the European negotiators. As a result, the figures for the European deficits were scaled down by several billions, namely, to about $22 billion over the four-year period.

Did we squeeze the water or the blood out of the Paris project, a newspaper commentator inquired? The answer is probably some of both. But it was clear to anyone that there were definite limits to American capabilities. Even though the dollar sign was used to fix the extent of European needs, clearly we were not to be asked to give dollars but American agricultural products, fuel, commodities, machinery, and other capital goods. America's supply of these was limited.

Here it may be well to clarify one point, and one that is clearly recognized in the CEEC report. The economic recovery of these countries depends primarily upon themselves. The ratio of the aid that we might give, if the Plan is carried out, to the total economic

2. *FRUS, 1947*, 3: 239.

3. William L. Clayton, at that time under secretary for economic affairs of the State Department, upon his return from the Geneva conference launching the General Agreement on Tariffs and Trade, wrote an influential memorandum to Secretary of State Marshall dated 27 May 1947. Marshall's assistant Charles E. Bohlen used phrases of this memorandum in writing Secretary Marshall's Harvard speech. See *FRUS, 1947*, 3: 230–32.

output of these countries is startlingly small, even though it is vital, because *no* amount of domestic effort will *immediately* produce the needed imports of food and certain crucial commodities. The report submitted to Congress by President Truman with his message of December 19, 1947, which I refer to from time to time as the "executive report" puts it this way (p. 69):

> The full amount of aid proposed for the European countries would certainly amount to less than 5 percent of their aggregated national incomes over the next 4 years and it would probably be closer to 3 percent. Even the total imports Europe will need from all sources could scarcely amount to 15 percent of the national income of the importing area.... Thus the standard of living and the rate of economic development in Europe depend overwhelmingly upon European production and resources. Unless the people of Europe work hard and productively, unless European governments, businessmen, labor unions, and farmers organize production and exchange effectively, unless the right goods and services are produced, and unless European governments carry through vigorously their undertakings with respect to fiscal and monetary reforms, no amount of American aid can bring about recovery.[4]

The Paris conference initiated its work in full appreciation of these basic facts. The CEEC report of the sixteen powers was not by any means solely a request for aid. It also set forth what these countries proposed to do. And to the report were appended specific declarations from individual countries. As a result, we have at least moral commitments as to their programs of domestic economic reform and rehabilitation, programs to which the United States can properly hold the countries to which it extends its aid.

Here are some of the production goals they proposed to reach by the end of 1951: (a) prewar bread grain production and livestock to be restored; (b) coal production to reach 584 million tons yearly, an increase of 30 million tons over 1938; (c) electricity output to be expanded to reach two-thirds above that of prewar; (d) oil refining capacity to be increased by two and one-half times prewar; (e) crude steel production to be increased to 55 million tons yearly or 20 percent above prewar. In addition, by 1951 they were to expand inland transport by 25 percent, restore their merchant fleets and arrange so that after the transition period they would

---

4. Only preliminary mimeographed copies of the report (see Dulles's "Introduction" in the Appendix), later printed for the use of the Senate Foreign Relations Committee (see footnote 38, chapter 2), were available when Dulles wrote the manuscript. Page numbers provided by Dulles thus do not correspond with the page numbering in the published report.

supply from European production the capital equipment needed for further expansion. Thus precise goals, translated into figures, were fixed. It is an ambitious program.

In addition, the report of the sixteen set forth certain general undertakings to which these countries committed themselves: (1) The creation and maintenance of internal financial stability; (2) the development of economic cooperation to bring production to the specified targets, especially in the cases of food and coal; (3) cooperation in the reduction of tariffs and trade barriers; and (4) organization of the means by which common resources can be developed in partnership.

These points deserve special mention, and first in order [is] the stabilization of currencies. Except for some of the neutrals, Switzerland in particular, the currency of most European countries is greatly overvalued in terms of the official dollar exchange. This means that there has been an artificial stimulation of imports and a drag on exports. Further, this overvaluation has had dire effects in the field of agriculture. The farmer has no incentive either to produce large crops or to turn over those crops to a government agency at government prices. Grain fed to hogs can be translated into greater value than if sold for an inflated paper currency at pegged government prices. Bitter as it may be for those who live on salaries or wages – or for any government – the time is overdue for the revaluation of most European currencies in terms of realities, that is to say, in terms at which in a free market these currencies sell in relation to stable currencies, such as the dollar or the Swiss franc. On December 15, 1947 the pound sterling, with an official rate of $4.04, was purchasable in New York at $2.50; the French franc, with an official rate of 119 francs to the dollar, could be obtained at the rate of 265. The Italian lira was even more out of line with reality, until it was unpegged in late 1947 and allowed to find its own level, which was then fixed by the government periodically as the official rate. For example, the rate for December 1947 was fixed at 603 [lira] to the dollar, which could be changed from month to month if a black market rate developed.

This currency situation brought out once again the truth of Gresham's law that bad currency drives out good.[5] The amount of gold and dollars that is hidden in the stockings of the peasants on the continent of Europe can only be guessed, but certainly it is a

5. Gresham's law, named after Sir Thomas Gresham, financial agent of Queen Elizabeth I, realized in 1558 that if two coins have the same nominal value but are made of metals of unequal value, the cheaper coin will drive the other out of circulation.

formidable figure and no mere threats by government can bring it out of hiding. Only restoration of buying power to the currency and the resultant public confidence can do it. Preliminary Report No. 2 of the Herter congressional committee,[6] which will be described below, has this interesting comment to make about the French "stocking and mattress" reserves:

> Other factors in addition to those mentioned in this report are present in France today which show the latent possibilities of a French recovery more rapid than its present aspect might indicate. Some estimates of gold hoarded in France run from $2,000,000,000 to $3,400,000,000. Obviously, no accurate figures are possible. If one includes the probable French share in the Swiss-held total of $800,000,000 worth of United States securities and at least $500,000,000 of French privately held assets in the United States, which have not been declared, there is a substantial supply of funds privately owned which could be brought out to help in the restoration of French and European prosperity. The condition of bringing out of hiding such hoardings within and outside of France is the restoration of confidence in the value of the French franc and in the political future of that country. Although this may not be fully achieved in the near future, a very substantial part of these holdings may be available for aiding European recovery if the recovery of France proceeds at a reasonable rate in the next year. It is not safe, however, to gamble on this in the 6 months' interim aid period.[7]

Certainly revaluation of currencies and stabilization would stimulate exports, increase the agricultures' return and bring some hidden capital into normal channels. Until some hope was rekindled by Secretary Marshall's initiative, most European countries were loath to talk of this matter. Without some prospect of achieving a balance between exports and those imports which had to be paid for in hard currencies, stabilization would be futile. It would only mean continuing revaluations and devaluations. If aid is given under the Marshall Plan, there is a chance that such balance can be achieved, and then some stability can be given to the currencies.

6. Christan A. Herter introduced a House resolution that provided for the appointment of a Select Committee on Foreign Aid to undertake an in-depth study of foreign aid. The committee was to determine the present and future requirements for relief and rehabilitation for foreign countries. For background information, the committee went on a fact-finding trip to Europe. When it ceased to operate in May 1948, the Herter committee had created twenty-four preliminary reports and supplements in addition to a final report.

7. These preliminary reports were later revised and incorporated in U.S. House of Representatives, Select Committee on Foreign Aid, *Final Report on Foreign Aid* (Washington, D.C., 1948).

Today the chaotic currency situation in Europe is one of the greatest obstacles to recovery. The honest suffer and the black marketeer is enriched. Currency smuggling has become a profession. Exports from many countries are priced at several times their real value, and overseas markets are slipping. What sometimes is not realized in the United States is that the facts of this situation are just as apparent to the governments of France and Italy as they are to the American columnists and economic pundits.

This whole subject of stabilization looms large in the report of the sixteen. They recognize that in most of the countries there is a surplus of purchasing power and too little to buy, thus creating a great stimulus to inflation. They recognize also that the success of their program to put Europe on its feet depends in no small measure on the restoration of internal economic and monetary stability. Accordingly, all of the countries represented at Paris which are suffering from inflation pledged themselves to carry out stabilization programs, and France, in particular, gave assurances that a comprehensive plan for economic and monetary stabilization would be submitted to an early session of the parliament. A similar pledge by the Italian government has already in part been carried out by the drastic revaluation of the currency which I have mentioned.

As sound financial practices, budget balancing and stabilization are absolutely essential if any aid from America is to be effective; the United States would certainly be entitled to hold the European countries to the promises that they have given. It is far more in their interests than it is in ours.

The CEEC report points out in connection with stabilization that the gold and hard currency reserves of the majority of the participating countries have been drained and that to restore confidence in these currencies in connection with a revaluation it may be necessary to strengthen the reserves. If the currencies of these countries are to be stabilized and made convertible, it was suggested that a $3 billion stabilization fund might be required.

Confidence in currency is mysterious and elusive. If economic policies remain chaotic, then a $3 billion currency reserve would go out the window almost overnight and it would be useless to give it. If, on the other hand, budgets are balanced and essential imports covered and currencies revalued, the resulting confidence might bring out of hiding in Europe more than three billions of gold and hard exchange. Certainly some additions to the gold and dollar reserves of the countries which boldly stabilize would aid in holding confidence once equilibrium is achieved. Today, however, it would hardly be equitable to suggest that this additional burden should be passed on to the American taxpayer, particularly as the United States has recently appropriated and paid in to the International Monetary Fund $2.75 billion to aid in world currency stabilization.*

Some interesting figures are given in the above mentioned executive report as to the estimated reserves of the participating countries. According to this report, the gold and short-term dollar assets of these countries as a group totaled $8.8 billion as of June 30, 1947. During the previous eighteen months these assets had declined more than $4 billion, and since June 30, 1947 the decline had continued at an accelerated rate and amounted to $700 million in the third quarter of 1947 alone. At the rate these assets were being dissipated, they would not hold out for *two more years*. Furthermore, this total of $8.8 billion is somewhat misleading, as it includes the reserves of the neutrals and $2.4 billion alone represents the reserves of Switzerland, Portugal, and Turkey, which remain more or less static.

In addition to these short-term, or what we might call currency reserve assets, the executive report estimated that the participating countries had long-term dollar assets of approximately $4.9 billion. The United Kingdom, the Netherlands, Switzerland, and France, the report stated, were the only countries which had any appreciable amount of these holdings. For the most part, of course, these assets were held by the nationals and not by the governments of these countries. In many cases the latter were not in a position effectively to realize on these assets, which, the executive report (p. 103) remarks, "provide current income annually to Europe and help to this extent to reduce the balance-of-payments deficit. In some instances also these assets may be important to the continuation of established international business relationships." Our government, undoubtedly recognizing how essential the retention of these slender assets might be, added in the report a significant comment: "With respect to both long- and short-term dollar assets the position has been taken that liquidation of these assets by the participating countries should not in general be regarded as a prerequisite for the extension of United States assistance."

The issue of stabilization and currency reform has an important place in the CEEC report. Equally important is what they have to

---

*. See Harriman report [President's Committee on Foreign Aid, *European Recovery and American Aid* (Washington, D.C., 1947) submitted 7 November 1947; for a summary of the report, see Department of State, *Bulletin* 17 (16 November 1947): 937–41, 948], p. 93.

say about building up a larger free trade area in Europe. The sixteen governments declared their recognition of the advantages of moving toward a customs union. They point out, however, that this is not something which can be accomplished "by a stroke of the pen. A Customs Union, particularly between several large and highly industrialised countries, involves complex technical negotiations and adjustments which can only be achieved by progressive stages over a period of years." The governments of Belgium, the Netherlands, Luxembourg, the so-called Benelux countries, have already taken a long step in this direction and propose to "conclude an economic union." The Scandinavian countries are making progress in the same direction. Thirteen of the sixteen countries represented at Paris have created a study group to examine the problems involved and the steps to be taken in the formation of a customs union between any or all of them. Preliminary meetings [have] already taken place.[8]

Here is evidence that Europe is roused to the fact that small, closely compartmented sovereignties, with customs barriers, as well as quota and currency restrictions, have little chance of enduring in the world today. They are moving and moving fast in the direction which may yet mean that out of the tragedy of World War II a closer union, something approaching a United States of Europe, may develop.

There was one important European state which was not physically present at the Paris conference but which like a ghost, haunted the deliberations of the sixteen. This was Germany. In a way, Germany was indirectly represented since the army commanders of the western zones had submitted detailed reports on the situation in their areas for the guidance of the conferees. The Harriman report (p. 117) likens Germany's position in Europe to that of the industrial district in the United States which extends from western Pennsylvania to Illinois, and remarks, "If the industrial production of this area were by some calamity reduced by half, it will be obvious to everyone that the economic life of the rest of the United States would be profoundly affected." Hence one can appreciate the impact on Europe of the fact that the index of production of the Bizone of Germany (that is the British and American zones of occupation) in July 1947 stood at 35 percent of 1938 levels.

The CEEC report frankly recognizes that the recovery of Europe is impossible without an economic recovery in Germany. "In particular, the output of the Ruhr coalfield, which is essential

8. Department of State, *Committee of European Co-operation: Volume I*, 34.

to the European economy as a whole, must not again be used by Germany in such a way as to constitute a threat to European security, but must contribute to the rehabilitation and economic stability of the whole of Europe, including Germany herself." The report goes on to say that "Other Western European countries cannot be prosperous as long as the economy of the Western Zone is paralyzed, and a substantial increase of output there will be required if Europe is to become independent of outside support." Recognizing that the population of the Bizone in 1951 will be from eight to ten millions larger than prewar, the report states that this area must increase its international trade above its prewar volume in order to meet minimum food and raw material requirements. "It is essential that the participating countries and Western Germany should both be able to pay their way after 1951: if either achieves viability only at the expense of the other, the European economy will still be unsound." It is a tribute to the French delegates, and an answer to those who claim that France will not permit German recovery, that France, as well as Germany's other neighbors, the Netherlands and Belgium, who suffered so much at Germany's hands, should have joined in recognizing this.[9]

Neither in dealing with Germany nor with their own problems did the conference of the sixteen make any attempt to gloss over the difficulties of the situation. The European economic "machine," the CEEC report admits, "was highly developed and delicate. It depended for its efficient working upon the smooth working of international trade and the uninterrupted flow of goods and services." All this the war broke down. Allied victory was obtained at the price of the destruction of many centers of production and the dislocation of the transport system. Shipping and foreign investments, upon which exports depended, were heavily sacrificed. Agriculture, trade, and industry "had been twisted out of shape," and 1945 found Europe "perhaps more denuded of resources than at any time in modern history." Inflation and the problem of unbalanced budgets, rising prices, and especially the scarcity of dollars, added to the bedevilment of the situation. Temporary improvement in 1945 and 1946 was nullified by the serious setbacks during the winter of 1946–1947 and the droughts that followed. The trend turned. Reconstruction credits were drained and the opening chapter of the report concludes, "the crisis is deepening, and its repercussions are spreading to every corner of the world [economy]."[10]

9. Ibid., Appendix B, "Problems Relating to Germany," 69, 70.
10. Ibid., 5, 6, 10.

The report then examined the basic needs of Europe. Among the striking figures it sets forth are these: Annual coal production in Western Europe was 113 million tons less than in 1938 – and here is one of Europe's major deficits. Crude steel production, again comparing 1938 with 1947, is off one-third, or some 15 million tons. The figures for grain production in certain countries are even more devastating. France, which before the war produced 8.9 million tons of bread grains annually, has fallen to an estimated 3.8 million tons for the 1947 harvest; Italy from 7.4 million tons to 4.7 million tons. These figures, of course, spell starvation without outside aid on a large scale because France, at best in good years, was just self-supporting and Italy was short of it. With crops ranging from slightly under to sightly over 50 percent of normal in these two countries, it is clear that domestic production will provide grain only for about six months of local consumption.

To meet what the conference of the sixteen conceived to be their minimum net import requirements for the calendar year 1948 – the largest items comprising food, fuel, fertilizer, and commodities such as cotton – approximately $8 billion was needed. This figure included $918 million for equipment other than agriculture and mining machinery. Of this total, $2.63 billion was said to be needed by the United Kingdom, $1.76 billion by France, $1.15 billion by the Bizone of Germany and slightly less than $1 billion by Italy. The requirements of the other countries scaled down in this order: [the] Netherlands $630 million, Greece $510 million, Belgium $320 million, Denmark $210 million, French zone of Germany $120 million, Sweden $150 million, and Norway $50 million.

This figure of approximately $8 billion is the estimated deficit of Western Europe with the American continent, not with the United States alone. It is not suggested that it could all come from the United States, but, by and large, it would all have to be paid for in hard currencies of one form or another, or in exports. Canada has already strained its credit by generous loans to Britain, largely for grain, but how far Canada can be expected to provide the dollars to purchase grain is a question. South America can furnish vital commodities including grain, but Argentina, the great grain producer of South America and one of the relatively low-cost producers in the world, has fixed a dollar price for its wheat more than *three times* that of Canada and almost *double* that of the United States. It is difficult to avoid the conclusion that members of the Argentine government are profiteering in human misery.

While a major burden will fall on the United States, others

should be called upon for help. For example, the report suggests that 20 million tons of cereal will be needed for Europe in the first year of the Plan. Of this, it is hoped that some 8 to 9 million tons (about 300 million bushels) would come from the United States. Most of the balance would have to be supplied from Canada and Argentina. The report recognizes, however, that the food in the world just won't go around, "there is not enough food in the world" to give Europe anything approaching its pre-war diet.[11]

The hard facts of the situation bear this out. Total world food production is sharply below that of prewar, whereas the population of the world has increased by some 200 millions. The Food and Agriculture Organization of the United Nations (FAO)[12] estimates the 1947–1948 food production, taking all the basic foods – grains, fats and oils, sugar, meat, dairy products, and potatoes – as averaging 93 percent of prewar and the population as averaging 108 percent of prewar. They estimate further that there is an unfilled gap of some 10 million tons in grain supplies. In addition to these actual shortages, there has been a breakdown of transportation facilities and a maldistribution of available foods in many parts of the world. This means actual famine in certain areas and such a shortage of food in others as to threaten political stability.

Many specific requests of the CEEC obviously could not be fulfilled. Agricultural machinery, for example, which is one of Europe's greatest needs. Help here would in time cut down Europe's need for grain imports, but the total of the CEEC request would take approximately one-third of the 1946 production of the United States, whereas our normal export has never exceeded about 15 percent of production to all sources. Further, certain of the American types of agricultural machinery are not economical for the small European farms. Hence, this item of the CEEC estimates is expected to be cut by about 50 percent from $1.2 billion to approximately $600 million for the four-year period. Germany, which was the great European supplier of this machinery, must be brought back as a major producer. In disposing of farm equipment, the French government might try an interesting experiment of which we could be part beneficiaries. If farm equipment made available under the Marshall Plan was offered in priority to those French farmers who would pay, say, 50 percent of the cost in dollars, the balance in local currency, the gold and dollars in the

11. Ibid., 49.
12. The Food and Agriculture Organization of the United Nations was founded on 16 October 1945 to raise levels of nutrition and standards of living and, as a final goal, to eliminate hunger.

stockings might come out. The farmers are probably ready to put their hidden gold and dollars into circulation if they can get something that is of value to them – and, after all, who can blame them for acting thus?

In their report, the sixteen make an urgent plea for adequate help in 1948. The program must be got under way with enough impetus to turn the tide. If so, the deficits in succeeding years can be reduced. The total of the hard currency needs over the four-year period 1948–51 is estimated in the CEEC report at $22.4 billion. Starting with $8 billion the first year, dropping to $6.35 billions in 1949, to $4.65 billions in 1950, and to $3.40 billions in 1951. Thereafter, the report concludes, somewhat optimistically perhaps, the European powers assume that any deficit with the American continent can be covered by the increase in their own imports.

While it is interesting to look at figures for years after 1948, they are largely meaningless. God and the weather, Stalin, Molotov & Co., the changing level of prices, and any number of other considerations, including internal politics, can alter for better or for worse the estimates made or the possibility of our meeting them. For the next six months, or at least until we see the next harvest and the next whim of Russian policy, one can judge with fair accuracy the vitally pressing needs. The attitude of Russia is important because the conclusions of the CEEC report are predicated upon the resumption of trade between Eastern and Western Europe, with the flow of cereals from Eastern Europe restored to prewar levels and with timber reaching 75 percent of those levels by 1951. If these somewhat optimistic hopes are not realized, the balance of payment position of the West European powers is not likely to be as rosy in 1951 as they hope.

The CEEC report ends with a warning:

> The Committee now submits its proposal for the necessary restorative action on the European side by production, stabilization and cooperation between the participating countries, as well as by measures to stimulate the free flow of goods and services. These proposals are reinforced by definite and specific undertakings by each of the countries concerned. But these undertakings can be successfully carried out only with the assurance of a continued flow of goods from the American Continent [sic]; if that flow should cease the results would be calamitous. Europe's dollar resources are running low. One country after another is already being forced by lack of dollars to cut down vital imports of food and raw materials from the American continent. If nothing is done a catastrophe will develop as stocks become exhaust-

ed. If too little is done, and if it is done too late, it will be impossible to provide the momentum needed to get the programme under way. Life in Europe will become increasingly unstable and uncertain; industries will grind to a gradual halt for lack of materials and fuel, and the food supply of Europe will diminish and begin to disappear.[13]

Those who have studied European conditions at first hand and who have analyzed the figures – the economic debits and credits – can hardly quarrel with this conclusion. What can the United States do? What should we do?

13. Department of State, *Committee of European Co-operation: Volume I*, 60.

CHAPTER 4

The United States Prepares
Its Answer

It was not necessary for the United States to await the CEEC report in order to know the basic facts of the European situation. Washington was almost as well acquainted with them as the conferees in Paris themselves. The story had been coming in for weeks from every capital of Europe. The British loan was not working out as it had been hoped, even though the last desperate run on this loan, following the July 15 date when sterling again briefly became convertible, had not yet started.[1] The disaster suffered by the French and Italian harvests was no secret; neither was the British food and coal situation.

So while in Paris the conference of the sixteen sought to tell us what they could do to justify our aid, and while in Moscow the Soviet hastily took up the attack, preparing a backfire of revolt, riot and sabotage, work was started in Washington to define the limits within which aid was possible.

We had, it is true, passed the initiative to the sixteen powers. Decisions on our part would not be necessary unless they could agree and reduce their agreement to a concrete proposition. But once they had done that, the success or failure of the Marshall Plan, and perhaps the future of West European civilization itself, might depend on the sureness and speed of our action. The United States was indeed strong, but how strong? It could help,

1. In December 1945, Great Britain had received a low-interest loan of $3.75 billion to cover short-term payment problems. After an increase in exports in 1946, the British financial situation deteriorated in late 1946. Mounting trade deficits, expensive domestic programs of the Labour government, increasing expenses abroad, and reduced income forced the British to draw on the loan more rapidly than had been anticipated. When the Bristish currency, the pound sterling, became convertible for a short period (July to August 1947), the rest of the loan was rapidly spent. The payments deficit actually increased by 50 percent until the summer of 1947.

but with what and how much? What were its resources and capabilities in this critical period, and how far could we judge of our capabilities over the next few years?

For seven years the United States has had good harvests and in 1947 the greatest wheat crop in its history. If after seven fat years, according to Pharaoh's dream, there should be even one really lean crop year, the world effect might be catastrophic.

The democratic process began to function, not with totalitarian haste, but with purposeful deliberation. And the best brains in and out of government were called in to help. We deliberated not behind the walls of a city within a city but in preparation for the open forum of public consideration and debate.

This work developed along three lines: first, a study of American capabilities so that we would know what we could safely export without upsetting our own economy; second, an independent appraisal from our viewpoint of the European situation so that we would have our own facts and figures and not be forced to rely solely upon those furnished us by others as to Europe's condition; third, a study of how aid could be most effectively administered both from the point of view of protecting the American economy and of bringing the maximum assistance to Europe.

It is important at the outset to have a clear conception of what we mean when we talk about aid to Europe. We are often deluded by the frequent use of the dollar sign and we talk loosely of making available so many billion dollars worth of aid. The dollars in themselves are only tokens; they are a call upon American goods so long as we permit their export. That is equally true, whether those dollars are used to buy goods in the United States for direct shipment to Europe or are loaned to a third country, Canada, for example, to finance wheat shipments to Europe. Dollars, in the last analysis, can only be spent in the United States, and even if they are in the hands of a third state which is not seeking aid, they represent a call upon our productive capacity. It would therefore be utterly futile and meaningless to lend them or give them away to an amount in excess of the goods which we can safely export.

When Mr. Bevin suggested that our gold reserve in Fort Knox might more usefully be employed by being distributed among certain other countries, he was, in effect, stating that it might be useful for the United States to distribute an amount of our goods represented by the value of that gold. In fact, it would be quite useless to take the trouble to move the gold as, under present world conditions, it would merely flow back to us as the means of purchasing our goods.

Right here it might be well to add a word as to one argument which is a favorite refrain of Moscow propaganda, namely, that, in order to protect ourselves against the threat of a depression and to keep the wheels of industry going here, we must find some way of distributing our goods abroad. The Harriman committee, referred to below, has this to say about that particular canard[:]

> The Committee regards as nonsense the idea which prevails to a considerable degree in this country and abroad that we need to export our goods and services as free gifts, to insure our own prosperity. On the contrary, we are convinced that the immediate economic danger to the United States is inflation, which means, among other things, a shortage of goods in relation to demand.[2]

The question of the safe limits of American aid to foreign countries was discussed in detail in a letter which ex-President Herbert Hoover[3] addressed to Senator Bridges,[4] chairman of the Senate Appropriations Committee on June [15], 1947. He pointed out that the greatest danger to all civilization would be for the United States to impair its own economy by drains which would cripple productivity: "Unless this one remaining Gibraltar of economic strength is maintained, chaos will be inevitable over the whole world." And he concluded, that "as the result of our rate of giving and lending we are overexporting goods and cannot continue at such a rate with our present production and consumption without further evil consequences to our stability."[5]

Obviously, this was a matter which deserved the most careful consideration and, on June 22, 1947, three weeks before the Paris conference met, President Truman appointed three committees to study the question of American capabilities and resource[s] as well as other phases of the Marshall Plan. One committee, composed of government specialists under the chairmanship of the secretary of the interior, Julius A. Krug, was particularly to study the state of our nation's resources. A second committee, the Council of Economic Advisers under the chairmanship of Edward G. Nourse, was to study the impact on our economy of aid to other countries. The third committee, under the chairmanship of the

2. President's Committee on Foreign Aid, *European Recovery*, 3.

3. Herbert Hoover had been president of the United States from 1929 to 1933. He chaired the President's Economic Mission to Germany and Austria. The Hoover commission's final report, arguing that German economic restoration was necessary for European rehabilitation, dated 18 March 1947, was released on 23 March 1947.

4. Senator Styles Bridges (Republican, New Hampshire).

5. The text of the letter is reprinted in *New York Times*, 16 June 1947, 4.

secretary of commerce, W. Averell Harriman, and including in its membership leaders in finance, business, farming, and labor,[6] was to study the broader aspects of the aid program and to advise "on the limits within which the United States may safely and wisely plan to extend" assistance to foreign countries.[7]

The Krug committee, in its report released October 19, 1947, recognized "the dynamic potentialities of the American economy, its capacity for growth and change," and stated that our present "unprecedented economic activity has resulted in the attainment of a gross national product, or total value of final goods and services produced or in process, of 204 billion dollars in 1946 and at a rate of 225 billion dollars annually for the first 6 months of 1947." Despite this great production effort, it was necessary to record the existence of shortage in many products resulting from the high rate of consumption.[8]

On the whole, the Krug report reflecting the administration viewpoint was encouraging as to our ability to supply many of the key materials required for Europe. The wheat crop of 1947, 1.4 [b]illion bushels, was more than 500 million bushels above the ten-year average for 1936–45 and "vastly in excess of our domestic food requirements."[9] Whether we could safely exceed in 1947–48 the preceding year's total of exports of about 10.5 million tons (approximately 400 million bushels) was doubtful in view of the short corn crop and the necessity for a substantial carry-over due to less rosy prospects for the coming harvest (1948). The exports of nitrogen, the committee found, did not constitute a significant drain on the resources of the country, but a reduced transportation cost was desirable and hence the production of nitrogen in Europe should be stepped up.

The amount of coal we might be asked to export was considered insignificant in terms of the resources of the United States, but here transportation and port facilities were stated to be bottlenecks. Steel, the Krug report remarks, is in many ways the most troublesome problem of all. On the other hand, exports of farm equipment will not create any substantial drain on our raw material resources, but there are bad shortages in many types of industrial equipment, particularly freight cars and mining machinery.

6. For a list of the Harriman committee members, see page 59.
7. Truman's statement upon creating the committees to study the relationship between foreign aid programs and the domestic economy, on 22 June 1947, is reprinted in Department of State, *Bulletin* 17 (5 October 1947): 691.
8. U.S. Department of the Interior, *National Resources and Foreign Aid: Report of J.A. Krug, Secretary of the Interior, October 9, 1947* (Washington, D.C., 1947) 2, 3.
9. Ibid., 5.

As to petroleum products, the need for the conservation of our own diminishing oil resources points to the desirability of our own importation of petroleum from abroad, and the desirability of building up these imports at least to balance any exports we may send to Europe.

The Krug report recognizes that we could make a substantial contribution to Europe, but its conclusions are all too general in character to permit any very precise figures as to the safe amount of exports in any particular category.

The second report, also from an administration agency, came from the Council of Economic Advisers. The council was created under the Employment Act of 1946 and is a part of the executive office of the president. There are three members of the council: Chairman Edwin G. Nourse, former director of the Brookings Institut[ion], Leon Keyserling, and John D. Clark. Describing the council in *The New York Times* of January 4, 1948, Cabell Phillips writes that it "represents a nice balance between the conservative economic doctrines of the National Association of Manufacturers and the progressive philosophy of the New Deal....Today virtually no decision from the White House is announced until the council has screened it for its economic impact."[10] The report of the council, generally referred to as the Nourse report, was made public by the president on November 1, 1947.[11] In dealing with the impact of foreign aid upon our own economy, the Nourse report recalled that in 1946 our exports totalled $15.3 billion and there was an export surplus of $8.1 billion. In 1947 we will have an estimated export surplus of more than $10 billion, or an increase of approximately $2 billion over 1946. In the second quarter of 1947 the United States export surplus with the rest of the world reached a peak at an annual rate of $13 billion. In that period United States exports were running at the rate of $21 billion and imports at the rate of $8 billion. The Nourse report points out that under the schedule of the Paris committee [the CEEC] the export surpluses would be somewhat less rather than greater than we reached during 1947 and concludes that "the general impact of a new foreign aid program of the assumed size upon the American economy could be sustained because a larger impact had already been sustained." This somewhat optimistic conclusion is not shared by all

10. *New York Times*, 4 January 1948, 9, 25–27. The quotation is from ibid., 26–27.
11. The report by the Council of Economic Advisors, entitled *The Impact of Foreign Aid Upon the Domestic Economy: A Report to the President,* is dated October 1947. It was submitted to President Truman on 28 October 1947. For a summary of the report, see Department of State, *Bulletin* 17 (16 November 1947): 932–35.

experts, some of whom consider our rate of export in 1947 as excessive. Further, the Nourse report qualifies its conclusions by pointing out that the problems raised by specific commodities in short supply could distort the picture, and that the "foreign aid program compels us to face certain domestic problems squarely, but remedial and preventive measures available to us are adequate if we have the courage to use them."[12] Here the controversial issue of "controls" raises its ugly head.

It was the Harriman committee which gave the most comprehensive consideration to the whole European aid problem. It analyzed the CEEC report and discussed European conditions in detail. Recognizing that, as to all years after 1948, any estimates are altogether speculative, the committee concluded that, whereas the CEEC report suggested that the four-year European foreign exchange deficit for 1948–51 would be about $22 billion, the Harriman committee estimated it would range from $17 billion to $23 billion. Making deduction for various types of financing other than government appropriations – for example, financing by the International Bank, the Export-Import Bank and commercial banks – it was estimated that the amount which Congress might be called upon to appropriate if the Plan were carried out would be between $12 billion and $17 billion over the four-year period. However, the Harriman report emphasized that aid must be extended to Europe on a year-to-year basis – no one could see ahead into the future. The committee briefly summarized its conclusions as follows:

1. The hope of Western Europe depends primarily on the industry and straight thinking of its own people.
2. The United States has a vital interest – humanitarian, economic, strategic, and political – in helping the participating countries to achieve economic recovery.
3. The aid which the United States gives will impose definite sacrifice on this country.
4. The magnitude of Western Europe's deficit with the American Continent in 1948 will be of the order of $7 billions, but when all possibilities of financing are taken into consideration, the approximate need for appropriations past and future to cover the calendar year of 1948 may be on the order of $5.75 billions.
5. The extension of such aid, now or in the future, calls for anti-inflationary fiscal policies on the part of this country, and a new agency to administer the aid extended.

As a final word, both on the magnitude of the program recommend-

12. Council of Economic Advisors, *The Impact of Foreign Aid* 75, 80.

ed and on the policies outlined, it is well to bear in mind that success depends on giving way neither to over-optimism or to undue pessimism. It is one thing to propose a program, it is another to see it through. The immediate months and indeed years ahead are not apt to be easy either for this country or for the European nations. It is not wise to underestimate the steepness of the climb.

By the same token, however, it is essential to maintain perspective. The years following World War I were years of intense dislocation and dissolution both at home and abroad. Yet, by 1924, Europe, which seemed totally disorganized in 1919, was well on its way to recovery. Even more in point would seem to be the wartime experience of this nation and other democracies. In 1940, it seemed inevitable that a large part of what we call Western civilization was irreparably lost. In late 1941, following Pearl Harbor, the fortunes of this nation were at an all-time ebb. Yet four years later, complete victory had been gained, American arms stood triumphant in the East and in the West, and it was obvious that the United States had entered into a new period of power, prestige, and responsibility. The following years have contained many disappointments. Wartime alliances have melted away. Yet it is safe to say that at no time in history has there been more need for Western Europe and the United States to stand firmly together. And who will say that, if we apply to the making of the peace the same spirit which triumphed in war, we may not see an equally dramatic vindication of the ideals and principles of free men everywhere?[13]

To those who may be overly impressed by the criticisms of columnists or the pronunciamentos of stray economists or financiers, it is worth while to recall exactly who composed the Harriman committee so that one can give proper weight to their judgment as contrasted with that of the casual critic. Nineteen men served under the secretary of commerce. All of them except the chairman, were at the time private citizens, though many had at various times rendered important services for the government. Almost every section of the country was represented and the men were chosen from the fields of business, banking, and education. There were also outstanding leaders of labor, as well as experts in the fields of mining, shipping, and agriculture. And to answer those who say that the Marshall Plan is possibly a good political gesture but is impractical and unrealistic, I would call as my first witnesses to the contrary the hardheaded men of affairs listed below and cite the testimony from them which I have quoted above.

13. Department of State, *Bulletin*, 17 (16 November 1947): 948.

The Hon. W. Averell Harriman
Secretary of Commerce
Chairman

Hiland Batcheller, Pres[ident],
Allegheny-Ludlum Steel Corp.,
Pittsburgh, Pennsylvania.

Calvin B. Hoover, Dean
Graduate School,
Duke University,
Durham, North Carolina.

Robert Earle Buchanan, Dean,
Graduate College,
Iowa State College,
Ames, Iowa

Robert Koenig, Pres[ident],
Ayrshire Collieries Co.,
Indianapolis, Indiana.

W. Randolph Burgess,
Vice-Chairman,
National City Bank of N.Y.,
New York, N[ew] Y[ork].

Robert M. LaFollette, Jr.,
Washington, D.C.

James B. Carey, Secy-Treas.,
C. I. O.
Washington, D.C.

Edward S. Mason, Dean,
School of Public Administration
Harvard University,
Cambridge, Massachusetts.

John L. Collyer, Pres[ident],
B.F. Goodrich Company,
Akron, Ohio.

George Meany, Secy-Treas.,
American Federation of Labor,
Washington, D.C.

Granville Conway, Pres[ident],
Cosmopolitan Shipping Co., Inc.
New York, N[ew] Y[ork].

Harold G. Moulton, Pres[ident],
[The] Brookings Institution,
Washington, D.C.

Melville F. Coolbaugh,
Colorado School of Mines
Golden, Colorado.

William I. Myers, Dean,
College of Agriculture,
Cornell University,
Ithaca, New York.

Chester C. Davis, Pres[ident],
Federal Reserve Bank,
St. Louis, Missouri.

Robert Gordon Sproul, Pres[ident],
University of California,
Berkeley, California.

R.R. Deupree, Pres[ident],
Proctor & Gamble Co.,
Cincinnati, Ohio.

Owen D. Young,
Honorary Chairman of the
Board of Directors,
General Electric Company,
Van Hornesville, N[ew] Y[ork].

Paul G. Hoffman, Pres[ident],
Studebaker Corp.,
South Bend, Indiana.

As a commentary on the Russian propaganda and on domestic attacks on the Marshall Plan which describe it as a plot of Wall Street capitalists, it is interesting to note that prominent labor representatives on the Harriman committee were vigorous in their support of the European recovery program. On the other hand, the United States Chamber of Commerce has circulated to its members literature designed to work against the Plan.[14]

While the executive departments and their inside and outside advisers were studying American capabilities and preparing these reports, Congress was examining the situation on the spot. Its members realized that if aid was to be given to Europe their constituents throughout the country would want to know what the situation in Europe was really like. Was it necessary to give this aid? What would be accomplished by it?

Some 200 members of the Senate and the House of Representatives travelled to Europe in the summer and fall of 1947. Many of them went with special mandates to study particular problems, such, for example, as the effect of what we called the Voice of America[15] and the condition of deportees. Members of the appropriations committees, foreign affairs and foreign relations committees were on missions of more general character. They wanted to know at first hand whether Europe could justify the call it was about to make on us and whether the Congress could properly respond. One committee, in particular, deserves special mention – the Select Committee on Foreign Aid, generally known as the Herter committee because it was constituted as a result of the resolution introduced into the House by the able congressman from Massachusetts, Christian A. Herter, who became its vice-chairman. Its chairman was the experienced head of the Foreign Affairs committee of the House, Charles A. Eaton. The committee was to study the program of foreign aid, and its mandate was to report on the needs of foreign countries, the resources available within and without the United States to meet those needs, agencies existing or agencies which should be set up to deal with them, and measures to correlate the assistance [that] the United States can properly make without weakening its domestic economy.

I venture the judgment that no great issue in our foreign relations, arising in time of peace, has had more careful study than the

14. Dulles refers to Henry Hazlitt's book *Will Dollars Save the World?* (New York, 1947). See also below for Dulles' discussion of Hazlitt's arguments.

15. The State Department's propaganda radio program Voice of America broadcasted in twenty-two languages, mostly by shortwave band.

project to give effect to the Marshall proposal. Having worked as a legal consultant with the Herter committee, I can attest to its serious, thorough and nonpartisan approach. Members of the committee visited practically every country of Europe which had any substantial part in the Plan and even countries on the other side of the Iron Curtain. Upon their return to the United States they were able to present a series of most valuable reports, eleven in number, covering not only the conditions in various European countries as they saw them but also their particular views as to the manner in which aid could most effectively be administered. While at times the democratic process may seem to work slowly, we have here an example of how soundly it can work.

The completion of all the reports and studies I have mentioned above, most of which were already available by the second week of November 1947, prepared the way for the calling of a special session of Congress for November 17. Events were moving to a crisis in both France and Italy. Moscow realized that the crop failures in these two countries made them particularly weak links in the chain of the Marshall Plan unless the food and fuel situation could be met. If Congress waited to act until its regular session beginning in January 1948, actual aid could hardly reach the stricken countries until well on into the spring, and by that time their resources to buy food in the world market would have been exhausted by some weeks. And once the machine stops turning it takes all the more power to get it in motion again. Hungry people cannot very well wait a month or two for food. Stopgap aid would be necessary, as Congress could hardly be asked to decide overnight on a long-range program and provide the machinery to carry it out.

It was under these circumstances that Congress met in special session and the Committee on Foreign Relations of the Senate and the corresponding committee of the House received the report of Secretary Marshall. The total cost of the European Recovery Plan over the four-year period was estimated by the secretary at from $16 to $20 billion, an estimate which was close to that of the Harriman report. Secretary Marshall, by the way, had particularly requested that the Plan no longer bear his name but be called the European Recovery P[rogram] – ERP. But the secretary's modesty will probably not find much of an echo. Once labeled the Marshall Plan, it is likely to remain such in the minds of the people and in the pages of history.

State Department estimates placed the cost of the Plan for the months of April, May, and June, 1948 at slightly under $1.5 billion and for the fiscal year beginning July 1, 1948 at about $6 billion. The secretary then added, "The findings contained in the Krug report, the Nourse report and the Harriman report, together with the studies made by our interdepartmental committees, make it clear that a program in this order of magnitude can be safely undertaken by this country."[16]

For interim aid to France, Italy, and Austria, Secretary Marshall suggested a total of $597 million, France's share being $328 million, Italy's $227 million, and Austria's $42 million. Here time was of the essence and the secretary urged Congress not to wait upon action on interim aid to set up the procedure for the long-range program.

In concluding his presentation, Secretary Marshall set forth his philosophy and the choice which faced the United States:

> The automatic success of the program cannot be guaranteed. The imponderables are many. The risks are real. They are, however, risks which have been carefully calculated, and I believe the chances of success are good. There is convincing evidence that the peoples of western Europe want to preserve their free society and the heritage we share with them. To make that choice conclusive they need our assistance. It is in the American tradition to help. In helping them we will be helping ourselves – because in the larger sense our national interests coincide with those of a free and prosperous Europe.
>
> We must not fail to meet this inspiring challenge. We must not permit the free community of Europe to be extinguished. Should this occur it would be a tragedy for the world. It would impose incalculable burdens upon this country and force serious readjustments in our traditional way of life. One of our important freedoms – freedom of choice in both domestic and foreign affairs – would be drastically curtailed.
>
> Whether we like it or not, we find ourselves, our Nation, in a world position of vast responsibility. We can act for our own good by acting for the world's good.[17]

As Marshall was speaking these words the Soviet counterattack was being carried out. Strikes promptly broke out in Paris. One French cabinet fell, a new and stronger one was formed to meet the Communist threat. Troops had to be called out in France and also in Italy, where the Communists attempted by force to take over the city government in Milan. It was a race against time. Would food and relief arrive in time to prevent the battle going by default?

16. Secretary Marshall's statement before the joint session of the Senate Committee on Foreign Relations and the House Committee on Foreign Affairs, on 10 November 1947, is reprinted in Department of State, *Bulletin* 17 (23 November 1947): 967–72.

17. Ibid., 972.

CHAPTER 5

The Means to the End

There has been widespread criticism of the program, or lack of program, in our outlays for relief during the two and a half years which followed V-E Day. It is said that there was no comprehensive plan, bu[t] rather a good deal of wishful thinking and sloppy administration. Some of this criticism is justified, some of it exaggerated.

It is true that there was then no overall plan which recognized that we faced not merely a temporary emergency, as we hoped, but a major reconstruction job. As a matter of fact, UNRRA,[1] under its charter, could only deal with relief. The Bretton Woods organizations, the International Bank for Reconstruction and Development, generally called the World Bank, and the International Monetary Fund,[2] the chosen instruments for financing longer-range reconstruction projects and promoting financial stability were slow in getting under way. Also they had grave difficulties in securing adequate financial resources as the hard currency and dollar shortage became acute.

As the actual fighting war ended in Europe, it was not easy to get any clear appraisal of Europe's needs or of Russia's attitude, which so definitely affected the European situation. We knew that much of Germany's economy had been blasted to bits, that England, France, and Italy had suffered heavily. We knew also

1. United Nations Relief and Rehabilitation Administration, established 9 November 1943.
2. The UN Monetary and Financial Conference at Bretton Woods, NH (1 July to 22 July 1944), established the International Monetary Fund (IMF) to help stabilize currencies, and the International Bank for Reconstruction and Development (IBRD) to aid devastated countries. The United States contributed about a quarter of the $8.8 billion for the IMF, and about 35 percent of the $9.1 billion for the IBRD. The Soviet Union had been invited, but was not among the forty-four nations present.

that the peoples of these countries were desperately tired and undernourished and that, in the case of France and other occupied countries due to Nazi intrigue, and in the case of Italy due to the corroding effects of over twenty years of fascism, man had been set against man until the social structure of these countries had been warped out of shape. Liberation had not brought internal peace. For many countries the postwar years spelled greater economic hardships than the years of the war.

It was natural, therefore, to put the emphasis on relief and more or less inevitable to continue to use the organizations built up during the war. There was UNRRA to which the United States had appropriated $2.7 billion for distribution to the war-devastated countries of Europe and Asia. This was 72 percent of its operating budget. Of this, Italy and Greece received together the largest amount, nearly $700 million. Lend-lease aid continued until V-J Day, August 15, 1945,[3] and, in all, a total of over $3 billion in various forms of relief went to the Paris conference countries alone during the two years ending June 30, 1947.

It was loans and credits, however, which constituted the chief items of the immediate postwar program. There was the loan of $3.75 billion to the United Kingdom in 1946, $1.15 billion of Export-Import Bank credits to France, plus a credit of $342 million for the purchase of surplus property and merchant ships, and about $200 million to Italy for the same purpose. In addition, there were credits to cover civilian type lend-lease goods held at the end of the war and a post-UNRRA credit of over $300 million in May of 1947. The total American aid made available for the sixteen European countries (plus Western Germany, exclusive of occupation costs) over the two-year period prior to June 30, 1947, reached almost $10.5 billion, and, over and above this, in 1946 alone, it is estimated that private charity and personal remittances, that is, aid from nongovernmental sources, exceeded half a billion dollars. In late 1947 loans from the World Bank were made to France, the Netherlands and other of the sixteen countries.

President Truman in his message to Congress of December [19], 1947 estimates our aid to all countries, not the West European powers alone, at $15 billion, since the surrender of the Axis powers. This aid we have extended "in the forms of grants and loans, for aid to victims of war, to prevent starvation, disease, and suffering; to aid in the restoration of transportation and com-

3. Victory Japan Day, the date of the surrender of Japan.

munications; and to assist in rebuilding war-devastated economies."[4]

This is a formidable total. Certainly without it Europe today would not be in a position where one could even plan a long-term reconstruction project. It met a desperate postwar need, but did not have a decisive result in turning the tide and starting economic recovery. The day of the old type of intergovernmental loan, of uncoordinated relief and of UNRRA activities is over.

America has had considerable experience in relief operations, but a program of reconstruction and rehabilitation on the scale of the Marshall Plan is novel, not only to the United States but in world history. In the field of relief we can look back on notable achievements. The Commission for the Relief of Belgium under the able direction of ex-President Herbert Hoover in the days of our neutrality during World War I was a conspicuous example. Never was a relief job done more effectively under more trying circumstances. Following the first World War, the American Relief Administration (ARA),[5] under the same leadership, was a truly effective organization. It had unity of purpose and direction, under able men who had the knack of making the various European countries share their resources in an effective manner. Also, they knew how to get relief supplies quickly to the points of greatest need. Their job was relief and when this emergency was over they withdrew. But they helped to build up local initiative and resourcefulness which carried on.

Later, the League of Nations, with a series of rehabilitation loans to Germany, Austria, Hungary, and Bulgaria, all of which were floated privately in the financial markets of the world, showed that under proper safeguards and efficient administration a relatively small amount of money can go a long way toward changing economic trends and promoting recovery. All of these precedents are useful, but today we have a far greater task than in the period following World War I.

What are some of the lessons we could learn from this past experience and from the two and a half years since V-E Day? No two persons would judge them alike, but the following points seem to me to embody certain general principles applicable to the present situation which experience should have taught us.

4. Truman's special message to Congress on the Marshall Plan is reprinted in *Public Papers of the Presidents of the United States: Harry S. Truman, 1947* (Washington, D.C., 1963) 515–29.

5. ARA helped to alleviate famine and to fight typhus and other diseases in Europe and the Soviet Union. Hoover headed the Administration from 1918 to 1922.

1. Able administration is one of the keys to success. Money is the easiest thing in the world to waste.
2. Intergovernmental loans should be avoided. If the credit of the borrower is good enough to justify calling for repayment in dollars, the loan should be handled by institutions such as the World Bank, the Export-Import Bank or by private capital.
3. It is useless to seek repayment in dollars from countries which have no dollars and no prospects of an early balance between their exports and their import requirements. Emergency aid, therefore, should be largely in the form of grants, or at least on a basis which does not call for dollar repayment.
4. There is likely to be less waste, and it will be better for the American economy, if we do the purchasing and dispense emergency aid in kind rather than in cash. Thus we avoid competition by foreign countries in our markets with our own money, and can somewhat temper the price-inflationary aspect of a foreign aid program.
5. Long-term reconstruction programs, involving capital goods and equipment, should be handled as far as possible on a business basis and by organizations which can exercise some control over the use to which the money is put. Private capital should be encouraged to take part in the program and given reasonable security, if necessary by government guarantees. The experience and techniques of private industry should be utilized.
6. The emergency aid program and the reconstruction and capital goods program must be coordinated.
7. The countries receiving aid must have programs which will insure the efficient use of the aid given. They must put their own houses in order to the best of their abilities so that the aid given will have maximum effect.

Principles such as these have been emphasized in the various reports on the Marshall Plan which have been presented by President Truman, Secretary Marshall, and by the Harriman committee, as well as in the various reports of the Select Committee on Foreign Aid of the House of Representatives (the Herter committee). Also, they have in part been embodied in the pilot legislation on the Marshall Plan, the Foreign Aid Act of 1947, which provided for stopgap relief to France, Italy, Austria, and China, and which became law on December 17, 1947.

In dealing with a problem as complicated as the Marshall Plan, and one which has so many implications affecting our foreign policy, our domestic economy, and international finance, it is not surprising that there should be important and honest differences of opinion. It is unfortunate that we must debate these differences on the eve of a presidential election.

As the year 1948 opened and Congress prepared for the debate on the Marshall Plan, here, in brief, is how the situation stood on the crucial elements of that Plan.

1. How much will the Plan cost?

The report of the Committee on European Economic Cooperation (CEEC) had evaluated at $22.4 billion the dollar deficit of the participating countries with the American continent for the four-year period 1948–1951, taking prices as of July 1, 1947. This of course did not mean that they expected an appropriation by the United States Congress of this amount. Some of the aid, over $3 billion they hoped, would come from the World Bank, for the financing of which some provision had already been made. Private financing might furnish a part. Aid might come from Canada and certain of the South American countries and, in part at least, it was hoped, this aid would not call for American dollars.

The Harriman committee's estimate, comparable to that of the CEEC, placed the same dollar deficit within a range of $17 to $23 billion and, after making deductions for various types of other financing, they reached the conclusion that Congress might be called on to appropriate between $12 and $17 billion to do the job.

Secretary Marshall, in his statement to the congressional committees on November 10, 1947, estimated the needed congressional appropriation at $16 to $20 billion, and President Truman in his message to Congress of December 19, 1947 asked Congress to authorize the appropriation of $17 billion over a four-year period. The executive report submitted to Congress with President Truman's message of December 19, 1947, stated, "The magnitude of needed United States assistance is estimated to range between 15.1 billion and 17.8 billion dollars."[6] Or $15.9 billion to $18.6 billion, if we include the approximately $800 million extra funds requested by the army for Germany – the so-called "disease and unrest" funds. These estimates show that, while experts differ, even experts in the same branch of the government, there is a measure of agreement as to the general range of the need.

Neither the Herter committee nor any other congressional body had given any overall dollar cost estimate prior to the January

6. Department of State, *Outline of a European Recovery Program*, 36.

1948 meeting of Congress. It was not, of course, proposed that Congress should immediately appropriate any such sum as $17 billion and President Truman did not suggest this in his message. What he asked was that Congress evidence its intention of carrying out the program on a scale which might reach $17 billion over the four-year period and hence sought an authorization of this amount. As laymen not acquainted with the intricacies of our congressional system do not always realize, authorizing legislation does not usually carry an appropriation. First comes the authorization, and then, unless Congress alters its mind, an appropriation is made. It is now generally recognized that Congress will appropriate for the Marshall Plan only on an annual or some other periodic basis.

We did not have to wait long for the answer. On January 6, 1948, an exchange of correspondence between Senator Vandenberg and the State Department was given out. The senator suggested the elimination from the president's project of legislation of the $17 billion figure and its replacement with the following language:

> There are hereby authorized to be appropriated to the President from time to time, out of money in the Treasury and not otherwise appropriated, such sums as may be necessary to carry out the provisions and accomplish the purposes of this act etc.[7]

Senator Vandenberg pointed out that one Congress could not bind another and that any global amount suggested today might be misleading: "The effective test each year is the Congressional appropriation – and there is no other." Furthermore, he said, any overall figure now is nothing more than an "educated guess."[8] The president readily accepted Senator Vandenberg's suggestion. But would Congress commit itself in principle to the idea of a global sum, and, if so, how much?

Today no one can predict with assurance either that $17 billion will be required or that even this great sum will do the job. I assume that the president in originally suggesting a global figure had a twofold purpose in mind. First, to give the European countries some assurance that we have serious intentions of carrying on for a considerable period of time; that we will not start the job and then turn aside. It is well to remember that these European countries in committing themselves to work with us, are taking

---

7. Vandenberg had made his letter to Secretary Marshall and a reply by Robert Lovett to Vandenberg public at a news conference on 5 January 1948. See *New York Times*, 6 January 1948, 1.
8. Ibid.

certain risks as well as becoming eligible for certain benefits. Many of them are next-door neighbors of Russia, and all of them are much nearer to Russia than we. Today Russian forces stand in the Soviet zone of Germany only eighty-five miles from the Rhine and only about 150 miles from the French, Belgian, and Dutch frontiers. What Russia thinks about the Marshall Plan and about those who have declared their willingness to cooperate within its framework is well known. Hence, some assurance to the European countries of our fixed intention of carrying on is an important element in the success of the Plan.

The second reason for seeking Congress'[s] authorization of a global figure is to obviate the necessity of debating every year the whole issue whether we are going ahead at all. If a global figure were authorized, it would then only be necessary to secure periodic appropriations within the limits of the total authorized and in the light of the needs as the Plan unfolds.

The figure of $17 billion furnishes a target for the opponents of the Plan and gives concern to many of its friends. Seeking to reduce the sum to comprehensible proportions, the former indulge in a game which might be called "argument by arithmetic." Thus the sum is decried as being almost twice the annual appropriation for national defense, as amounting to approximately half the annual government budget, or as constituting a "gift" to Europe of approximately $120 from every person in the United States. Pursuing this same technique further, the more captious critics vie with one another in seeking new items for comparison. They perform fascinating feats of computation, and then announce proudly the number of imaginary washing machines, or automobiles, or bathtubs – or mothballs – that could be purchased with an equally imaginary $17 billion.

The sum is vast. This is not even debatable, but it is certainly pertinent to remind those who are impressed with this specious form of argument that the sum is also less than the cost of three months of war, when, at the peak of our military expenditure, we were spending at the rate of $80 billion per year. Furthermore, as President Truman pointed out in his message of December 19, it is about 5 percent of the cost to the United States of World War II and will be less than 3 percent of our national income during the life of the program.

But all such comparisons are irrelevant to the issue. For, as indicated above, any such figure has value largely as an indication of the seriousness of our intentions. There is no price tag on chaos – or salvation. If we are to be realistic with ourselves and the world, we must recognize at the outset, whether or not we now fix a global sum, that it would be useless and a waste of money to start with the Plan unless we propose to carry it on for several years.

How much do we propose to spend in the first year of the Plan, or rather, during the fifteen months following April 1, 1948, when our interim aid will probably have been used up and when Britain will long since have finished the last $400 million of its $3.75 billion loan?

President Truman estimated the cost for this period at $6.8 billion (not including $822 million separately requested of Congress by the army department for its "prevention of disease and unrest in Bi-zonal Germany" program) and asked for early action to authorize and *appropriate* this sum. The CEEC, whose estimates covered calendar years rather than our fiscal years, estimated the total deficit of the participating countries with the American continent at about $8 billion for 1948. That committee added, "This is not stated in the report as a request for special aid to that extent, for some of the deficit may be covered by loans from the International Bank, private investment, or other means."[9] The Harriman committee estimated the 1948 deficit at $7 billion and fixed the need for appropriations to cover the calendar year 1948 at $5.75 billion, a figure very comparable to the $6.8 billion suggested by the president for the fifteen-month period April, 1948 to June 30, 1949.

Here again is a target for the opponents of the Plan, and probably a substantial share of the congressional battle will revolve around the first year's appropriation. It is worth while, therefore, to consider how these totals are reached.

They are based on the estimated amount which the various countries will require in food, fuel, and fertilizer, and in commodities such as cotton. To this is added the estimated cost of the materials, such as agricultural machinery, mining equipment, trucks, and the like, which may be needed to help put the economies of these countries on a going basis. Then dollar transportation costs are added. From this total is deducted the share of these requirements which can be obtained elsewhere than in dollar countries or which do not involve dollar costs and the amount of dollar assets available to the recipient countries from export trade or otherwise.

Estimates of food needs for the first six or eight months of 1948 are calculable within reasonable limits of error as we know about

9. Department of State, *Committee of European Co-operation: Volume I*, 59.

the last harvest. For the balance of the period they depend in the case of certain countries, particularly France and Italy, on the 1948 crops. In countries such as England, Belgium, and the Netherlands, import requirements of foodstuffs are more static, as the domestic food production furnishes at best only a relatively small part of the consumption. Fuel needs fluctuate somewhat, depending largely on British and Ruhr production, but within narrow limits can be computed. In any event, the European and American experts do not differ very widely as to the probable range of needs for food and fuel. But the foreign aid program is not a mere relief and feeding operation. It would be a waste of money merely to feed the European countries for a year or two and not give them the tools without which they would have little chance of righting their own economies. How large a quantity of these tools should be sent depends upon what we can safely spare and, within such limits, our judgment of what can be effectively used to quicken recovery. The cost of these tools and general estimates of quantity available for export can be estimated. In this way some estimate can be made of first-year requirements.

What we do in the first year of the Plan may be decisive. If the machine gets going with impetus, it may carry on with steadily reduced outside aid. If it starts lamely, or has to stop now and then, it is doubly costly to gain momentum. If you let the fire go out in a blast furnace it is an expensive job to restart it.

In the Congress there will undoubtedly be those who will advocate a two or a three billion dollar Marshall Plan for the initial period. And, playing upon the elements of uncertainty of any calculation, it will not be popular to send abroad what our people need here at home, not to speak of the legitimate pressure for tax reduction.

In this situation, I suggest that there is a possible basis for agreement which would meet those who honestly want to see the job done and yet have real difficulty in deciding what is the correct amount to appropriate. Of course, with those who really wish to destroy the Plan by starving it out there is no basis for compromise.

Congress, instead of making an appropriation to cover the fiscal year ending June 30, 1949, might appropriate a lump sum of money as capital for a Marshall Plan administering corporation and authorize the corporation to draw against the Treasury up to this stated amount, without definitely tying the corporation down as to the period over which that money would be spent. Then, let us entrust the corporation's management to a man and a business-trained board of directors who enjoy the full confidence of the executive and of Congress, and I mean both parties in Congress. I believe such a man and such a board could be found. The corporation should then have freedom to spend the money over such period as the management of the corporation considers essential to the inauguration of the enterprise. And let us add a measure of continuing congressional control, namely, that the corporation would report through the president to a joint committee of the Senate and the House at stated, say quarterly, intervals, so that the Congress could currently judge what was going on. If the money was not being wisely spent, if results were not being achieved, Congress, as the master of the nation's purse, could at any time take action to cut off or to adjust future drawings on the treasury even below the limits of the total original authorization. At least six months before the date when it is estimated that the corporation's funds would be exhausted, Congress would be asked to consider replenishing them.

It is true that this would introduce an element of uncertainty, but unless the expenditure under the Marshall Plan is such as to hold the backing of the Congress, it would be cut off in any event after the first annual appropriation was exhausted. Certainly, it is better to have a flexible formula which will provide adequate funds to get the program under way, with Congress reserving the right to control all along the way, than to start with what may be a totally inadequate appropriation so that each and every operation has to be scaled down below the point of efficiency.

Many government projects of this nature, such as the Reconstruction Finance Corporation[10] and the Export-Import Bank, have worked on this basis. They could not have operated on the fiscal year theory. I doubt whether any business enterprise in the United States could successfully carry on if tied down to rigid twelve-month periods. It is hampering and unnatural for a type of undertaking like the Marshall Plan. In the long run, it is costly.

The Herter committee (report No. 8) suggests a program somewhat along these lines[:]

> The original capital of the corporation should be an amount sufficient to cover estimated operations to June 30, 1949. As of December 31,

---

10. The Reconstruction Finance Corporation had already been chartered in 1932 and was authorized to lend money to banks, railroads, and other institutions. Hoover had tried to obstruct the creation of the corporation. Only weakly financed with a capital of $500 million and the authority to borrow additional $2 billion, it turned out to be ineffective in the economic and social crisis of the Great Depression. Roosevelt adapted it to the New Deal and increased its capital resources and extended its responsibilities.

1948, and semiannually thereafter, the corporation should present a full financial report to the Congress, showing the disposition of its capital funds and the estimated amounts needed to make good any capital impairment, in order to permit the Congress to review the operations of the corporation, exercise its right to modify or abolish it, or to consider any further appropriation to its capital. This would maintain congressional control, within the limits prescribed over the funds of the corporation and yet would give the corporation reasonable scope within which to formulate plans of sufficient duration to permit the recipient countries to develop their own programs of reconstruction and recovery.

I shall revert to this point below in considering the type of agency which should run the Marshall Plan.

2. What do we contribute?

In first line, it will be food, fuel, and fertilizer, to keep body and soul together, so that there will be men and women in Europe with the strength and the will to work. And then they will be given some of the tools so that they can increase their own production of food, fuel, and fertilizer. This means farm implements, mining machinery, trucks, and transportation equipment. Also, there will be certain commodities needed, particularly cotton. And with it all, some incentive goods, such, for example, as tobacco. On page 74 there is a table indicating the goods that Europe might import from the United States over the four-year and three months period of the Plan. This table is furnished in the executive report (p. 177) and includes most of the items which might enter into a program for delivery under ERP, but does not appear to be exhaustive.

Of course, it is only a general estimate – much depends upon future crops and upon a close analysis of what items prove to be the most effective in promoting recovery as the Plan develops.

The second phase of the Plan, but one to be carried on concurrently with the aid program, covers the longer-range task of reconstruction – the capital goods needed to rehabilitate industry, to restore power plants, transportation and harbor facilities, and the like. This, it is hoped, will be largely financed through the World Bank, the Export-Import Bank and by private capital.

To encourage private capital, the President in the executive report suggested that a certain amount of the funds appropriated – a ceiling of 5 percent was proposed – should be made available to guarantee reconstruction loans by private capital. The government was not to underwrite the ordinary business risks, such as the

Estimate by the Executive of Value of Selected Imports of the
Participating Countries from the United States,
April 1, 1947 to July 1, 1952,
on the Basis of July 1, 1947 Prices.*

COMMODITY	APRIL–JUNE 1948	1948–1949	1949–1950	1950–1951	1951–1952	TOTAL
1. Bread Grains	218.3	535.5	509.7	411.6	411.6	2086.7
2. Coarse Grains	5.8	82.9	120.0	133.0	133.0	474.7
3. Fats and Oils	20.0	80.4	88.0	97.4	97.4	383.2
4. Oilcake and Meal	4.4	17.7	22.6	22.6	27.1	94.4
5. Sugar	6.5	21.4	17.3	10.5	11.0	66.7
6. Meat	1.7	6.0	12.1	17.9	23.8	61.5
7. Dairy Products	75.2	160.0	105.7	101.5	90.3	532.7
8. Eggs	12.0	24.0	12.0	12.0	12.0	72.0
9. Dried Fruits	6.9	26.6	25.2	17.6	20.0	96.3
10. Rice	1.1	6.1	6.1	6.1	11.9	31.3
11. Other Foods	9.2	64.6	61.2	80.4	80.4	295.8
12. Tobacco	52.5	210.0	217.4	215.6	215.6	911.1
13. Cotton	142.5	438.3	437.6	458.7	480.5	1957.6
14. Nitrogen	2.4	14.0	7.8	–	–	24.2
15. Phosphates	.6	2.5	2.5	2.5	2.5	10.6
16. Agricultural Machinery	–	136.3	161.5	131.8	115.5	545.1
17. Coal	92.3	297.0	135.1	49.6	24.9	598.9
18. Coal Mining Machinery	–	81.9	52.7	37.6	34.5	206.7
19. Petroleum**	121.3	530.6	546.2	570.5	537.0	2305.6
20. Timber	24.0	96.3	93.1	88.0	76.4	377.8
21. Finished Steel	44.6	182.1	186.9	179.3	126.6	719.5
22. Crude and Semifinished	11.9	47.2	47.2	47.2	43.5	197.0
23. Pig Iron	.3	1.3	1.3	–	–	2.9
24. Scrap	.4	1.6	–	–	–	2.0
25. Trucks	19.7	80.9	40.1	33.9	33.6	208.2
26. Freight Cars	–	60.0	18.0	–	–	78.0
27. Steel Equipment	–	48.1	48.2	48.2	48.2	192.7
28. Timber Equipment	–	16.9	22.2	11.7	11.7	62.5
29. Electrical Equipment	=	95.0	100.7	85.0	65.0	345.7
Total	873.6	3365.2	3098.4	2870.2	2734.0	12941.[4]

* This table is taken from the "Outline of a European Recovery Program," which was submitted to the Congress by President Truman with his message of 19 December 1947 [Department of State, *Outline of a European Recovery Program*, 115]. It is generally referred to in the text as the "executive report."

** Total imports from dollar sources, largely outside the continental United States.

local insolvency of the debtor, but the transfer into dollars of the debtor's assets in an amount sufficient to pay the loan if the debtor was solvent. This ceiling of 5 percent seems rather on the low side if it is really desired, as it should be, to link private business with the carrying out of the Plan on a decisive scale.

The Export-Import Bank will also be available to finance shipments of commodities, particularly cotton. And this type of financing can sometimes be arranged even in the case of countries, Germany for example, which today have scant dollar resources. Cotton can be sent to the mills of Germany and enough of the finished cloth sold abroad in hard currency countries to recoup the amount of the original loan. The country of manufacture would retain a part of the finished material and would also keep its looms working.

The president and Secretary Marshall, the Harriman and Herter committees all are in general agreement that there are two closely integrated phases of the recovery program; the grant in aid and the reconstruction loan programs. Here is the way Secretary Marshall stated the case to the congressional committees on November 10, 1947:

> where need is clearly demonstrated and where repayment cannot reasonably be expected, imports of supplies which are quickly consumed, such as food, fertilizer, and fuel, of indispensable items of capital equipment for immediate replacement and repair, and of essential raw materials should be financed by means of grants. Loans should be made to cover imports of capital equipment and raw materials which will directly produce the means of repayment and where such repayment can reasonably be expected. At the same time every encouragement should be given to early initiation of private financing so as to eliminate as far as possible the necessity for direct assistance from the U.S. Government. Use should also be made of the resources of the International Bank whenever in the opinion of the Bank the necessary and appropriate conditions for loans can be met.[11]

President Truman in his message to Congress of December 19, 1947 emphasized that the aid for which he was requesting appropriations from Congress included grain for current consumption and fertilizer and agricultural machinery to increase European production; fuel for current use and mining machinery to increase the coal output; in addition, there were to be raw materials, such as cotton, and some manufacturing and transportation equipment to increase productive capacity. "The industrial goods we supply

11. Department of State, *Bulletin* 17 (23 November 1947): 969.

will be primarily to relieve critical shortages at a few strategic points which are now curtailing the great productive powers of Europe's industrial system."[12]

How much of the total effort falls within the relief – grant in aid – category and how much could be handled by rehabilitation loans? The two merge together, as already suggested. Some commodities may have to be handled by way of grant and some on a basis of repayment. The same is true of some of the equipment and raw materials.

The executive report stated that the determination as to whether aid should be in the form of grants or loans would depend upon the capacity of each country to pay and the effect of debt accumulation upon its recovery. The report added, "The determination in each case, so far as funds provided by the Congress are concerned, should be made by the administering agency with the advice of the Department of State and the National Advisory Council on International Monetary and Financial Problems (NAC)." Then the interesting suggestion is added that where it is decided that loans are appropriate, the funds should be allocated by the Marshall Plan agency "to the Export-Import Bank of Washington, which should make and administer the loans as directed by the administering agency in consultation with the National Advisory Council."[13] The National Advisory Council, presided over by the secretary of the treasury and including the secretary of state, the secretary of commerce, the chairman of the Board of Governors of the Federal Reserve System and the chairman of the board of the Export-Import Bank, was organized pursuant to the Bretton Woods Agreement Act to coordinate the international financial and monetary policies of the United States and the operations of American representatives on the World Bank, the International Monetary Fund, the Export-Import Bank and other like agencies. Under the president's proposals, the NAC is to play a substantial role in determining financial policy under the Marshall Plan.

Analyzing the figures of European import requirements as supplied by the CEEC, the Herter committee (report no. 9) divided the total aid which might be sought from the United States into four categories and reached the following conclusions: Over the four-year period 1948–1951, 42 percent of these requirements consists of food, fuel, and fertilizer, 27 percent of other raw materials

---

12. *Public Papers: Harry S. Truman 1947*, 521.
13. Department of State, *Outline of a European Recovery Program*, 46.

and 25 percent of capital equipment. six percent is labelled as miscellaneous. If one takes the total import requirements of these countries from the entire world, 70 percent falls within the food, fuel, and fertilizer category and only 30 percent in the other categories.

Analyzing the selected imports given in the table on page 74 above, we reach slightly different results, as this table except for petroleum, covers goods and commodities of United States origin and not the total that might be financed under a Marshall Plan, including what is purchased in foreign countries. The important items in this table and their respective percentages of the total are food 33 percent; fuel 22 percent; cotton 15 percent; agricultural and mining machinery and transportation equipment 8 percent; iron and steel 7 percent; tobacco 7 percent; miscellaneous equipment 5 percent; miscellaneous 3 percent.

Presumably, practically all the food, fuel, and fertilizer category would be handled through the Marshall Plan agency and also a certain percentage, possibly initially about one-half, of the raw material and equipment categories. On this basis, about 70 percent of the total reconstruction program would have to be covered by appropriations and grants in aid, and the balance of around 30 percent, it is hoped, could be financed through the World Bank, the Export-Import Bank and through private channels. It will, of course, be important that the Marshall Plan agency which, in the first year, will bear at least two-thirds of the burden, should work in the closest coordination with the other government agencies and with private capital, which may finance a part of the program. There must be a consistent and coordinated recovery plan. The two sections of it cannot be clearly differentiated; they will overlap at many points and in every country which will require our aid. There is no use in giving food without the tools for recovery, and the tools for recovery, unless people are in a condition to use them, would be of little avail.

3. Who would get the aid?

No official attempt has yet been made to decide how much any one of the particular countries might receive under any Marshall Plan. This could only be determined when appropriations are made and individual needs analyzed. The condition of crops, the rate of coal production, and many other factors must be taken into account. However, the CEEC has given us a breakdown of the estimated dollar deficit with the American continent of nine of the principal participating countries for the year 1948. This gives us a clue as to their views of the respective needs.

There were sixteen countries in all in the CEEC. Of these, the neutrals – Switzerland, Sweden, Eire, Portugal – will not expect any emergency grants, and Iceland's needs are few. Certain of these countries will have a surplus and should be on the *giving* rather than on the *receiving* end. Where, as in the case of Sweden, there is a temporary exchange difficulty, due largely to an expensive attempt to buy Soviet good will, the need should be met by private financing.

This leaves only eleven West European countries as possible petitioners for emergency aid. Nine of these eleven (and the three zones of Germany) – that is, all but Austria and Turkey – furnished the estimates I mentioned above. If we accept these estimates as giving a rough approximation of the relative needs of the respective countries and make adjustment for the absence of Austria and Turkey, as well as for the fact that Turkey and Greece received special aid, we reach the following results: Britain, France, the three zones of Germany, and Italy will probably require between 75 percent and 80 percent of the total aid furnished, somewhat in these proportions: Britain 30 percent, France 20 percent, Germany 15 percent, and Italy 12 percent. The Netherlands and Belgium will require approximately 10 percent of the balance, with the needs of the Netherlands exceeding those of Belgium in view of the war damage which she suffered and the temporary dislocation of [the] Netherlands['s] economy due to the troubled trade relations with the East Indies. Austria, Norway, and Denmark, together with Greece and Turkey, would account for the balance, the amount of aid going to Greece and Turkey being a question mark until we know the results of the substantial allocation made to these two countries in 1947. How successful they are in the employment of the present grant should certainly be an important criterion in determining their qualifications for further aid under the Marshall Plan.

In determining the states to which aid may be sent, we should not fall into the error of neglecting our friends who have made an impressive start toward recovery, merely because their present needs are possibly less than those of others. There should be rewards, not penalties, for sound fiscal and economic policies. Take countries such as Belgium and the Netherlands, for example. Under [the] most difficult circumstances both have shown us what can be accomplished by determination and good planning.

4. Under what conditions will the aid be given?

The countries which are to receive our aid have already outlined in the CEEC report what they themselves propose to do in the way of internal reform to make our aid effective. Certainly it would involve no interference in their internal affairs if we held them to their own assurances, voluntarily given.

In his address to Congress President Truman noted that the Paris conference nations had "pledged themselves to take specific individual and cooperative action to accomplish genuine recovery."[14] In consequence of this, and following the precedent which was embodied in the Interim Aid Act, he recommended that each of the countries receiving aid would be expected to enter into an agreement with the United States pledging itself to take action along the following lines:

(a to increase industrial and agricultural power,
(b) to stabilize currencies, establish proper rates of exchange and restore confidence in the monetary system,
(c) to reduce trade barriers,
(d) to make efficient use of aid received "within the framework of a joint program for European recovery ... in the interest of European economic recovery,"
(e) to stimulate the production of specified raw materials and the procurement of such raw materials by the United States for stockpiling purposes,
(f) to deposit in a special account the amount of local currency equivalent to the aid furnished in the form of grants, such deposits to be used in a manner mutually agreed upon between the United States and the country concerned,
(g) to give full information regarding the use to which our aid is put.

After enumerating these points, the president added that few would "retain the right to determine whether aid to any country is to be continued if our previous assistance has not been used effectively."[15]

No mention is made in this enumeration of the kind of social structure the several countries should maintain. We do not tell them what sort of government they should have or what we would do if they decided to nationalize an industry. To do this would be construed abroad as direct political interference in their domestic affairs.

14. *Public Papers: Harry S. Truman, 1947*, 522.
15. Ibid.

When the Foreign Aid Act of 1947, which covered aid for France, Italy, Austria, and China, was under discussion in the House, an amendment was proposed to the effect that the extension of aid should be terminated if it is going to countries whose governments become dominated by Communists or by the USSR. In the measure as passed, no such provision was included, and discretion was left to the president to terminate aid "whenever he finds that because of changed conditions aid under the Act is no longer consistent with the national interests of the United States."[16] The wisdom of leaving this discretion is, I believe, apparent on analysis. It might be difficult to judge whether a particular government was dominated by Communists or not; the government of Czechoslovakia, for example. In any event that government does not today qualify under the Marshall Plan and the legislation leaves ample authority to stop aid whenever our interests require it.

In connection with the agreements to be negotiated with the various countries which will receive our aid, there is one point which needs to be stressed. It is not desirable that we should deal with each of the European countries as separate watertight compartments. This would only strengthen the separatist tendencies among them. The slogan "Europe must federate or perish," which many European statesmen have endorsed, must not be forgotten. The aid which we may furnish under the Marshall Plan might afford, with skillful handling, the strongest incentive toward a greater degree of unity in Europe.

The European countries must be brought to appreciate that this is a European program, that we are not giving aid to Britain and to France and to Italy as separate entities, but that we are endeavoring to promote West European recovery. It is important that we should not permit the unity of purpose which was evidenced in the really dramatic conference of the sixteen European powers in Paris in the summer of 1947 to disintegrate. Separate agreements are necessary, but I would suggest that we endeavor to have an overall master agreement to which all would be parties and which would set forth their united purpose to work together among themselves and with us to accomplish their objective of unity.

Each and every one of the points which the President suggested for inclusion in bilateral agreements constitutes a principle which concerns all of the European countries, and they should unite together and with us in solemnly proclaiming them. Then, once

16. Section 6 (c) of the Foreign Assistance Act of 1947, printed in U.S., *Statutes at Large, 1947* 61, part 1 (Washington, D.C., 1948): 934–39.

we have this master agreement, we could have, under its aegis, separate agreements relating to the particular conditions affecting each country that may receive aid, because on certain of the details, and particularly as to the amounts, there will be differences between them.

The Paris meeting did not adjourn *sine die*. It remains in effect a continuing conference, and this was one of the bold decisions made in Paris. Let us not allow it to disintegrate. Here our influence is vitally needed.

5. What will we get for our aid?

Under this heading I propose to discuss tangibles, not intangibles. Not what we will receive in the form of national security and national well-being, but what we can expect to receive in cash or other tangible assets.

The general form of the program has been indicated in earlier pages. Sixty percent to 70 percent of the total ERP program will cover food, fuel, fertilizer, light equipment, certain commodities. In the first year at least, this for the most part cannot be financed against payment in dollars or by granting dollar loans to the recipient countries. It will have to be given in kind, largely as grants, in the form of food and goods, not cash.

Of course, wherever dollars are obtainable, we should sell our produce, but among the CEEC countries, except for the neutrals, few could pay in dollars and the dollar obligations of these countries would be merely embarrassing scraps of paper to the giver as well as to the holder. They just could not be paid.

But outright gifts are unwise. We should not give away this nation's assets without obtaining in return what we can reasonably require from the receiving government. Also, no self-respecting country likes to be an object of charity and those which sink to the point of accepting this status are unlikely to have the incentive to change the comfortable position of being the recipient of charity.

A great deal of thought has been given to this problem and general agreement seems to have been reached that a country receiving aid from the United States and not giving us dollars or their dollar I.O.U. for this aid should set aside under special arrangements the countervalue in local currency of the aid it receives.

This idea of accepting local currencies in payment for our aid is not new to the proposed Marshall Plan legislation. Something of this nature was included in the so-called Post-UNRRA Aid Act (Public Law 84, 80th Congress), approved May 31, 1947, which authorized appropriations up to $350 million. Here the government of the receiving country was to agree that when it sold relief supplies for local currency, such local currency would be deposited in a special account which would be used within that country, subject to the approval of the United States, for relief purposes, including American expenses incident to the furnishing of the relief.

It is now felt that this formula could be considerably improved. When we ask that we get from the receiving country only the amounts they receive upon the sale of the goods, we tend to put a premium upon the giving away of these goods or their sale at less than full value. Further, these amounts are not always easy to determine. Hence, it is now suggested – and this provision is included in the Foreign Aid Act of 1947 – that we should receive a "commensurate" amount in local currency at the going rate of exchange of the value of the goods delivered, irrespective of the price at which they may eventually be sold. The receiving country shall undertake

> to make, when any commodity which is not furnished on terms of repayment in dollars is made available under this Act, a commensurate deposit in the currency of such country in a special account under such general terms and conditions as may, in said agreement, be agreed to between such country and the Government of the United States, and to hold or use such special account for, and only for, such purposes as may be agreed to between such country and the Government of the United States, and under agreement by the government of the receiving country that any unencumbered balance remaining in such account on June 30, 1948, will be disposed of within such country for such purposes as may, subject to approval by Act or joint resolution of the Congress, be agreed between such country and the Government of the United States.[17]

Here is the way this formula would normally work: The United States, for example, would deliver to, let us say, France, one million bushels of wheat, which we will assume had been purchased at a cost of three dollars a bushel, or a total cost of three million dollars. To that sum we would add any transportation charges which might have been paid by the United States. The total would then be computed in francs at the rate of exchange fixed by the International Monetary Fund, today approximately 119 to the dollar, making a total of some 360 million francs, plus the transportation charges. This sum would then be set aside in a special

19. Section 5 (b), printed in ibid.

account and would be used, as provided in the agreement negotiated between the United States and France. The same type of formula would apply to Britain, in the case of the British pound, to the Italian lira, etc.

This is a relatively simple formula under which to operate in computing in terms of local currency the value of the aid that is given. The receiving country would budget as an expense the cost of the aid in terms of its own currency. As a compensating item on the other side of the balance sheet, they would have the local currency proceeds from the sale of the goods received. Returning to our illustration of the one million bushels of grain, let us assume that this was milled into flour and then the flour was sold. The French government would receive in francs a certain amount for the flour. If this amount were equal to the cost of the grain plus the milling and handling charges, the amount received would cover the item they had budgeted and made available in local currency. If the flour or the bread were sold at a loss, as might well happen since all these governments must keep down the price of bread, the government would have to cover by taxes, assuming it was balancing its budget, the difference between what it received and the cost to it of the grain delivered by the United States.

Under this scheme very large amounts of local currencies would pile up. Amounts so large, in fact, as to have a very important effect upon the economy and the financial structure of the various countries concerned. This would raise a host of problems of a novel nature. The first and obvious question is that of ownership. Who will have title to the funds? Neither the president's message nor the Foreign Aid Act of 1947 gives a clear answer.

The Harriman committee has adopted the old formula of basing the local currency deposits on the receipts of the sale of goods furnished, but it goes on to suggest that these local currencies be held in "trust accounts," such accounts to be available "by mutual agreement of the United States and the country concerned only for certain specified purposes and with the understanding that their expenditure would not constitute a burden upon the foreign exchange of that country; that is, was not to be transferred into dollars." Among the uses to which funds would be put would be "the purchase of strategic raw materials which the United States desire to stock pile, and which could be obtained either in the country itself or its dependencies." The purposes would also include "expenditures to aid in the production of the strategic raw materials, or other local currency expenditures required by the United States government, such as expenditures for its embassy

or representatives, or expenditures for education or cultural purposes such as those specified in the Fulbright Act" (Harriman
report, pp. 92–93).

The Herter committee has given particular attention to these
local currency funds, and in the legislation submitted by Mr.
Herter (H[ouse of Representatives] R[esolution] 4579 [on 25
November 1947]) the matter is gone into carefully. After providing
that the new Marshall Plan agency could receive local currency
funds in payment where dollars or dollar obligations were not
forthcoming or appropriate, the legislation provided that they
should be handled as "local reconstruction funds" under arrangements with the various recipient countries to contribute "to the
rapid recovery of economic stability ... and of developing new
sources of wealth," and, in particular, (1) to be invested in securi-
ties of any "enterprises and projects which will contribute to such
recovery or develop new sources of wealth," (2) to acquire "strategic and critical materials for stockpiling in the United States, and
to develop natural resources for future stockpiling," (3) to promote enterprises of mutual interest to the United States and the
receiving country, and (4) to aid in furnishing technical assistance
to further the reconstruction efforts of the foreign country concerned.[18]

The legislation proposed by the Herter committee recognizes
the intricate nature of the problem of utilizing these local currency
funds in a constructive manner and without interfering with the
internal affairs of the various countries. Obviously, the Soviet
Union will pounce upon this proposal as being calculated to put
the various countries under the financial control of the United
States – making them the "49th state," as General Zhdanov, the
Cominform spokesman, remarked. There is no way of preventing
malicious criticism, but to avoid any real basis for the charge, the
draft Herter bill throws extensive safeguards around the use of
these funds in the interests of the receiving country: (1) We
should not exercise control over the management or operations of
any enterprise in which the funds are invested. (2) We should not
try to transfer the funds into dollars without the approval of the
International Monetary Fund. (3) We should do nothing to impair
the monetary or other fiscal policies of the receiving country.
Further, it is generally recognized in all the proposals on the subject that the funds should be used under agreements which will be
freely negotiated between the United States and each country

18. Pages 14–15 of the legislative bill to H.R. 4579.

where a fund has been set up. Here other safeguards could also be introduced.

The executive report suggested that these local currency funds might be put to any one or more of the following uses: (1) to assist financial reform and currency stabilization, (2) to retire national debt, (3) to defray local currency costs incident to the development of production of strategic materials, (4) to cover the local currency costs of projects sponsored by the World Bank, and (5) to meet the local currency costs of the American Economic Recovery Administration.

In the agreement negotiated between the United States and France, January 2, 1948, it is provided that a special account for these funds shall be created in the Banque de France in the name of "Credit National" and used for debt or currency retirement and agreed measures to promote stabilization. It is clear that this is only an interim solution of this difficult problem and that it will come up for further consideration when the long-range ERP plan is debated.

The various proposals regarding the local currency funds have brought out one suggestion which deserves to be further developed, namely, the possibility of using them to help us build up stockpiles of strategic materials. I have mentioned what the Harriman and Herter committees had to say on the point. The president's message to Congress of December 19, 1947 strikes a similar note. Each of the countries receiving aid, he said, will pledge itself, among other things, to "stimulate the production of specified raw materials, as may be mutually agreed upon, and to facilitate the procurement of such raw materials by the United States for stockpiling purposes from the excess above the reasonable domestic usage and commercial export requirements of the source country."[19]

If we try to use these local currency funds to buy up reserves of existing strategic materials from the Marshall Plan countries, we would be merely depriving them of foreign exchange, since any of these materials could be sold in the world market for cash. Not only that, but Western Europe does not produce metals and minerals in sufficient quantity to satisfy its own requirements and is to some extent competing with the United States for the exportable surpluses of Latin America and the British Dominions. Consequently, the homelands of the sixteen nations would not be able to assist us directly in this respect.

19. *Public Papers: Harry S. Truman, 1947,* 522.

However, the colonial territories of these countries have important undeveloped resources. Here production might be expanded so that the normal world markets would not be affected. The critical materials in the Herter committee's estimation include tin from the Far East; nickel, copper, lead and zinc from Canada; manganese, chrome ore and asbestos from South Africa; manganese and mica from India; cobalt and tin from Belgian Congo; and manganese from the Gold Coast. Of course, in many of these producing areas – Canada, for example – the local currency funds would not directly be usable. In certain areas, however, these funds might be put to some use and thus help to cushion private capital and encourage it to undertake new programs for developing the production of strategic materials.

That we have a national need for these strategic materials is already recognized. We don't propose to be caught again in another emergency where we are dependent on the maintenance of long sea lanes to reach supplies essential to our protection. The United States is already committed to a large-scale program for the stockpiling of strategic materials. This was done when Congress passed the National Resources Production Act in July 1946, which initially authorized $200 million. However, in the almost two years which have elapsed, little has been done under this legislation because of the heavy demands of industry for all kinds of metals during the reconversion period. As the Herter committee report No. 10 states, "large stockpiles can be accumulated only by expanding total world production." But they estimate that strategic materials for stockpiling might easily be obtainable up to a value of $200 million per annum from the dominions and colonies of the participating countries. At least it is well worth exploring whether these local currency funds which we propose to acquire in return for a part of our aid can play a role in furthering the expansion of world production of strategic materials.[20]

The Harriman report (p. 273), which devotes a special section to the stockpiling of strategic materials, confirms this judgment. "With comparatively small increases in production, which in most cases would require reaching but not exceeding wartime peak outputs, strategic mineral raw materials" valued at over $223 million annually could be made available.

The executive report adds th[ese] suggestion[s]: (1) Dollar funds made available under the Marshall Plan should be available

20. These preliminary reports were later revised and incorporated in U.S. House of Representatives, Select Committee on Foreign Aid, *Final Report on Foreign Aid* (Washington, D.C., 1948).

to finance the procurement of equipment and services required from the United States to increase the production of strategic materials; (2) the local currency funds should be available to cover local currency costs of such expansion; and (3) bilateral agreements should be made with the country within whose territory the strategic materials are being developed, so that the United States would get for stockpiling purposes a fair proportion of the strategic materials produced.

A new vista may be opening up in this respect. We should not take a defeatist attitude about the resources of the world. The great era of exploration and development which preceded World War I and which has been described in the first chapter of this book, is not necessarily at an end. Africa holds out great opportunities. Over the years, through exploration, development, reclamation, and the use of modern techniques in turning deserts into gardens, Africa may yet prove to be the salvation of a Europe that is starving for new sources of raw materials. America's skill and technique, its engineering and organizational genius, might well be linked with that of Europe. In this way we can help Europe to develop new resources for its own recovery, and Europe can help us by developing materials in short supply in the United States. Such a program, of course, cannot bring results overnight. It may take years. It is difficult to say at this moment to what extent these local currency funds could help, but if we furnish some initiative and capital, including a part of these local currency funds, we may both revive hope in Europe and rekindle the spirit of enterprise possessed by the pioneers of the British, French, Dutch and Belgian overseas empires. But we should go at it from the start with a greater regard for our social responsibility than some of the early buccaneers.

6. How will the program be administered in the United States?

The success or failure of the program will depend in large measure upon the methods of administration, both on the giving and on the receiving ends. We have within our own power the choice of the administrative machinery for procuring, allocating, and delivering supplies. In a sense, too, we have a right of review over the administration on the receiving end. If it is inefficient and wasteful, we should curtail further aid until the administrative defects are remedied.

That the executive and Congress are likely to look at these

administrative problems from different viewpoints is already apparent from the reception which was accorded the program outlined in the president's December 1947 message to Congress. To administer the recovery program, the president recommended the creation of a new organization "to provide central direction and leadership" and proposed the establishment of an Economic Cooperation Administration – ECA – to be headed by an administrator appointed by the president, responsible to him and confirmed by the Senate. He stressed that the relationship of the ECA to existing governmental establishments was of crucial importance, that it must work closely with the Department of State and with the other departments of government, particularly in the procurement and allocation of commodities in short supply.

The Harriman committee recommended that a new organization with centralized authority be set up to administer the program. It should have powers and form of organization such "as to make the job attractive to the most capable men in the United States." The corporate form of organization was suggested as the most flexible, and this corporation, it was urged, should be freed from the red tape incident to government departments. The heads of the various government departments directly concerned with foreign aid should be members of the board of the new corporation, including the secretary of state, who should "have a leading voice in the deliberations and policies of the new organization." The operating corporation was also to have an advisory group, consisting of representatives of the public, business, agriculture, and labor, with the task, among others, of helping to maintain public confidence "that the program was being carried on in a nonpartisan manner in the best interests of the country as a whole."[21]

The operations of the new agency, according to the Harriman report, would include checking and screening the requirements of the participating countries and the responsibility for the acquisition and delivery of supplies, taking into account not only what can be wisely and safely exported but "also the requirements needed to maintain the economics of other countries and to carry out our foreign policy in other parts of the world."[22]

The Harriman committee recommended that the new organization should not be empowered to decide the total amount of our exports of any particular commodity or what share of the total amount of exports should go to the participating countries as a whole. It could, however, determine how the total amount allocat-

21. President's Committee on Foreign Aid, *European Recovery*, 109, 110.
22. Ibid., 112.

ed to all participating countries should be divided among them. The new organization, under this Committee's scheme, should have the power to veto shipment to any participating country if it felt that such country was attempting to buy in our market materials or supplies which were not deemed essential for its recovery program. To achieve close cooperation between the new organization and Congress, a joint congressional committee on the pattern of the Atomic Energy Commission was recommended (Harriman report, pp. 105–114).

Like the Harriman committee, the Herter committee favored a new government agency – a corporation. The corporation is to be an independent agency of the United States with a chairman of the board and seven other directors appointed by the president. An equal number is to be taken from the two major political parties. Thus it is to be strictly a bipartisan, and hence, it is hoped, a non-partisan, organization. The chairman is to be a full-time employee, but this is not required of other directors.

To coordinate the policy of the new corporation – called Emergency Foreign Reconstruction Authority (EFRA) in the bill – with the executive departments of the government a separate Foreign Aid Council was provided for, consisting of the secretary of state as chairman, the secretaries of the treasury, national defense, agriculture and commerce, the directors of EFRA, the chairman of the Export-Import Bank and the American director on the World Bank. The two latter would be there to help coordinate the work of the World Bank and the Export-Import Bank with EFRA. The chairman of EFRA was to be the executive director of the Foreign Aid Council and, as such, was to formulate for its consideration the proposed programs of aid. Thus the Herter committee differed from the Harriman committee. The latter gave the executive departments direct representation on the board of the new corporation, whereas the Herter bill placed them on the policy council, the idea being that they should advise and determine overall policy but that the corporation would do the administering.

Rather sharp differences of views emerge from these three suggestions as to the American administrative machinery for handling the Marshall Plan. The executive viewpoint is that the new agency should function under the close supervision of the executive departments of the government, particularly the Department of State, and should operate largely through them. The viewpoint indicated in the Herter committee reports is that the new agency, while subject to policy directives in matters affecting foreign relations, should have a wide measure of independence and broad authority. The Harriman committee takes a middle position. It makes the governmental policy men, the secretary of state and certain cabinet officers, members of the board of the corporation rather than members of a separate advisory council, as was the case in recommendations of the Herter committee.

These differences will certainly be debated by Congress. Arthur Krock, in the *New York Times* of December 21, 1947, in fact, opened the debate in the press. He asserted that the machinery proposed by the president for the European recovery Plan "is designed from a model which became the symbol of inefficiency and waste during World War II.... The model is responsibility without authority."[23]

The carrying out of the Marshall Plan will be a major objective of foreign policy and, within the limitations fixed by Congress in the legislation setting up the Plan, the executive branch of the government must determine the broad lines of policy. The secretary of state, presumably, would determine the countries to which aid should be given, the political or other conditions under which it should be given and also probably, within reasonably flexible limits, the amounts which each country should receive. The broad lines of the agreements with the foreign countries certainly must have the approval of the secretary of state. We cannot have two people running the foreign policy of the United States. But within such general limitations as these, there is every reason to give wide authority to the man who will be chosen to administer the Plan. He must have a chance to do it without crippling restrictions of a bureaucratic nature.

Here we have the biggest job of economic reconstruction in history. If it is run along efficient business lines, it has a chance to succeed. If it becomes a political football, or if control of its administration becomes a matter of rivalry between departments of the government, it will be cruelly hampered. Certainly there are men in the United States of outstanding business ability who are outside of the push and pull of politics, who could be trusted to handle the task and who would be willing to do so if given the requisite authority. This is a field in which Americans have outstanding competence. Let us choose a man in whom we have confidence and hold him accountable to the president and the Congress but give him a chance to do the job. And let us hope that we will not get so tangled up in disputes as to how the job should be done that we do not do it at all.

23. *New York Times*, 21 December 1947, sec. IV, 3.

Certainly there is here a reasonable basis for a meeting of minds – one which will protect the integrity of our foreign policy and yet promote the efficiency of the administration of this great enterprise.

7. Where shall we purchase and how shall we ship?

The United States is no bottomless cornucopia of wealth, even though it stands today as by far the richest and most powerful country in the world. Even our great resources could be over-strained and a drop in the curve of production would be disastrous not only for Europe but for ourselves. The Soviet is confidently counting on this. In fact, we have already disappointed them by successfully passing over critical deadlines which they had advertised as the beginning of the great American depression.

Certain of the items which Europe requires, particularly machinery and machine tools, can today be acquired only in the United States. Many of the things which Europe wants are in short supply here, and it is recognized that we will have to maintain some export controls in order to protect our own economy and also to see to it that what is shipped abroad in the first instance goes to the country where the need is greatest.

It is therefore contemplated that the wartime controls which under existing legislation would largely lapse on leap-year day, February 29, 1948, should be extended. Whether these controls should remain where they are today, largely in the Department of Commerce, or be transferred to the new agency under the Marshall Plan has not yet been determined. The executive favors keeping them where they are. [T]he Herter draft legislation would turn them over to the head of the Marshall Plan agency on the theory that the handling of these controls will be essential to the administration of the relief program. Here a definite deadline for action has to be met, namely, February 29, 1948.

There are a couple of other political problems which must be resolved in drafting any new legislation. Should the new agency have the right to purchase supplies with dollars outside the United States and ship them to Europe, and, if so, under what conditions and to what extent? And, secondly, how should the goods be shipped?

The Foreign Aid Act of 1947 dealt with the first question and fixed certain principles to guide our purchasing policy: (1) Supplies could be purchased abroad when they could be acquired themselves there more cheaply. (2) 10 percent of the appropriation could be made available to purchase commodities outside of the United States, even though the cost be higher than the domestic cost, if the president finds that the particular commodities are in short supply in the United States. (3) Petroleum products shall be acquired outside the United States to the maximum extent practicable.

How will the commodities be shipped? The whole question of transportation is one of the most perplexing phases of the Marshall Plan, both because of the large costs involved and because here we run into several bottlenecks. We have been short of box cars to move grain and of open top cars to move coal, and, as far as transportation is concerned, grain and coal are the two most important items. For example, during the first half of 1947, according to the Harriman report, the total water-borne dry cargo exports from the United States were about 44 million tons and of these roughly 10 million tons were grain and 20 million tons were coal. Obviously, one way to cut down the staggering transportation costs of the aid program is to increase European coal production so that we can eliminate the uneconomical land and water transport of this bulky material.

Total transportation costs for the commodities proposed to be shipped to Europe from the Western Hemisphere under the Marshall Plan, as listed above, would cost, according to the executive report, approximately $1.44 billion in the period ending June 30, 1949, $950 million in 1949–50, $850 million in 1950–51, and $860 million in 1951–52, or a total of $4.1 billion. While the dollar sign is attached to these figures, this does not mean that any such huge sum of dollars will be required. The participating countries expect to perform, themselves, a large part of these services, and they have estimated that their gross outlay for dollar tonnage during the four-year period will be $1.7 billion, and this estimate is considerably scaled down in the Harriman report.

To find a solution of the transportation problem which will be economical, protect the American merchant marine, and promote a reasonable revival by the European powers, particularly Great Britain, of their role in the maritime carrying trade, would tax the wisdom of a Solomon. There has already been considerable criticism of the program of the CEEC, which contemplates a high level of merchant ship construction in Europe at a time when there are in fact a plethora of ships in the world, mostly in American hands. On October 1, 1947 there were one thousand dry cargo vessels in our laid-up fleet. At the same time, the European powers had under construction sixty-nine vessels which appeared to be duplications of vessels in long supply in the United States. Iron and steel, so critically short in Europe, seemed to be going where it was least, rather than most, needed. The European powers claim that the types of ships they are building are specialized for their particular trade needs; needs which could not be met by our *Liberty*, *Victory* or other wartime types.

The issue is not made more simple by the pressure of the American shipping interests for a monopoly of the shipment of American relief and reconstruction supplies. In fact, there is already legislative precedent whereby all such supplies must be shipped in American bottoms where available. Of course, where such supplies can be shipped in foreign vessels our dollar outlays could be reduced but not, of course, eliminated since bunkerage, insurance, and the like, would largely be dollar costs in any event.

Here we find ourselves torn between the vital necessity of maintaining and encouraging a merchant marine for our peacetime needs and as a safeguard for the emergency of war, and the desire to cut down the dollar costs of the ERP. We must recognize, however, that the recovery of Great Britain and of certain other West European countries, and their ability to pay their own way in the future, is tied in with their recovery as maritime nations. That recovery will spell increased competition for our own merchant marine. Here is a tangled issue which will require real statesmanship. We should face it boldly, for, as we start to restore Europe, we must recognize that we are building up competition for ourselves. If we are not prepared to meet healthy competition in the whole field of trade and commerce, the easiest thing in the world for us to do is to allow Europe to disintegrate. Then we might have only the competition of the Kremlin and a few with whom to trade.

This dilemma is inherent in the entire Marshall Plan. The Plan presupposes that we desire to help restore a Europe which can and will compete with us in the world markets and for that very reason will be able to buy substantial amounts of our own products. We cannot eliminate European competition and build up European purchasing power. We cannot monopolize the carrying trade of the world and have either an economically run Marshall Plan or a healthy Europe.

8. Government monopoly or private enterprise?

This general survey of the ways and means of carrying out the Marshall Plan raises one further question which deserves to be considered. Are we not helping to create here in the United States a vast government monopoly of foreign trade which will tend to eliminate the private enterprise system in the international field? The government at this end will procure and ship the supplies, and governments at the receiving end will be in the business of dispensing hundreds of millions of dollars worth of American produce.

There is no way that we can dispense with the intervention of governments in this program. But in working out the mechanics of the Plan we can introduce safeguards both to bring private enterprise here and abroad into the Plan at every possible stage and to provide for a transition from government to private channels as more normal conditions result. Private channels should be used on both the distributing and the receiving end as far as possible, and the purpose should be to build up private enterprise, not to destroy it – build it up both here and in Europe. One strong argument in favor of administering the Marshall Plan here through a corporation is that a corporation, even though government owned and financed, will have more of the ordinary business attributes than a mere government agency. It could more easily deal directly with private business interests abroad.

The administration has already approved in principle the idea that the ERP agency should guarantee the exchange risk in approved cases where private industry and private capital are prepared to handle specific projects. The Export-Import Bank in Washington has set an excellent example in its handling of loans. It has encouraged direct contact between private enterprise in the loaning and borrowing countries and has done its best to develop the ordinary channels of business. It is therefore heartening to note that under the administration plan the new ERP agency, where it extends credit and does not make goods directly available, will do so through the Export-Import Bank. This will enable the latter to apply its wide experience and acquired technique in seeing that these loans are handled on a business basis.

Under proper safeguards, the Marshall Plan need not build up any governmental octopus in the international field. Certainly there will be those in Congress who will be watchful on this point. The administration has already indicated that it recognizes the danger of attack from this angle, and in the executive report states:

> To the greatest extent possible, even at the start, and progressively as the program develops, the emphasis should be on the use of normal channels of trade and on meshing the program into the long-run objectives of freer multilateral world trade.... Private trade channels, both in

the supplying and the participating countries, should be used to the maximum extent practicable in the procurement of commodities under the European recovery program... Procurement should be returned to private channels whenever practicable.[24]

This chapter has given an outline of the shape and substance of a Marshall Plan as it stands at the beginning of 1948. It has sketched the areas of agreement and the important points of disagreement. It is well, as Senator Vandenberg insists, that this great project should be fully debated by Congress. It should be debated in the press and in the homes of our citizens from one end of the country to the other. It should be debated in no narrow spirit of partisanship, as was the Treaty of Versailles and the League of Nations in 1919. We have developed in world consciousness since those days, as we have shown by our support of the United Nations.

But we should not embark on a Marshall Plan program until we have counted the effort, the cost and the sacrifice that we are disposed to put into it. Our decision, once made, must then carry us along with sufficient momentum and over a sufficient period of time so that we can judge with some sureness the measure of our accomplishment.

---

24. Department of State, *Outline of a European Recovery Program*, 54-55.

CHAPTER 6

And Now for the Critics and Skeptics

F ew great enterprises have been undertaken in the course of history with an advance assurance of success. Certainly this is true of the Marshall Plan. The secretary himself remarked, "The automatic success of the program cannot be guaranteed.... The risks are real."[1] He added, however, that they were carefully calculated risks. Former Under Secretary of State Will Clayton, the undisclosed coauthor of the Marshall Plan,[2] has used much the same words, "success is not certain. This is a risky enterprise.... It is a task desperately difficult and complex. Most Americans, and even many Europeans, do not realize how close Europe is to a general breakdown."[3] Are we justified in taking this calculated risk, and what is the alternative? Let us see what the critics have to say about it.

The most pungent phrase of the skeptics is that the Marshall Plan is "Operation Rathole." They point to the fact that we have already expended or appropriated some $15 billion for relief and reconstruction since V-E Day and ask if we have accomplished anything by it. If these vast expenditures and appropriations have brought us today to a point where Europe is on the verge of collapse, how can we hope to save Europe by appropriations of money which, under any plan proposed, will probably be less on an annual basis than what we have been spending over the past two years?

1. Department of State, *Bulletin* 17 (23 November 1947): 972.
2. Clayton's memorandum to Secretary of State Marshall dated 27 May 1947, is reprinted in *FRUS, 1947* 3: 230–32. See also chapter 3, footnote 3.
3. "Is the Marshall Plan 'Operation Rathole'?" by Will Clayton as told by Beverly Smith, Washington editor of the *Saturday Evening Post, Saturday Evening Post,* 29 November 1947, 26–27, 137–38. The quote is from page 26.

No one claims that it is possible to give a sure and complete answer to this question. It cannot be said by anyone that $17 billion over four years, or any other sum, or the goods that such a sum represents, will "save" Europe. What one can say with complete assurance is this: If Western Europe does not receive substantial aid, there will be widespread starvation, even in this year 1948. There is also likely to be a breakdown in its economy and industrial life. Under these conditions, there is little hope of preserving these countries for what we call western civilization. They are likely to be reduced to the status of impotent minions of Russian communism. While the aid we have given in the past has not spelled recovery, it has brought Western Europe to the point where a plan of rehabilitation is a reasonable risk. It has brought Western Europe to a point, as 1948 opens, where it looks to the future with some hope, without which no plan can succeed.

After all, one can equally well ask whether World Wars I and II were "Operations Rathole." We have spent on the one more than $41 billion and on the other approximately $349 billion, and this does not take into account future billions in pensions and veterans aid. We did this to prevent the happening of events in Europe and in Asia exactly similar to those with which we are threatened today in the same areas. It is utterly futile today to speculate as to whether these investments of blood and money were wise or foolish. As an adult nation, we made them. The American people made them with their eyes open. And are we today to alter our course and refuse to make an investment of some 5 percent of the costs of these enterprises in trying to safeguard the objectives for which we fought? Should we now turn aside from the whole course of American history, which, as I shall develop later on, stems back not only to World Wars I and II but to the principles enunciated in the early days of the Republic?

Governor Dewey,[4] in a statement supporting the Marshall Plan, well stated the issue, "we have no choice today whether or not to act in this emergency. It is unthinkable that, after a successful war at staggering cost in blood and resources, we should now stop and surrender the fruits of victory. We will be doing just that if we permit the free nations to fall into economic chaos and then under Soviet control."[5]

And Senator Vandenberg, in an eloquent appeal to the Senate to

---

4. Republican Governor Thomas E. Dewey was to be the contender for the 1948 presidential election.

5. The text of the speech is reprinted in *New York Times*, 6 November 1947, 12.

pass the Foreign Aid Act of 1947, stressed the same issues. After describing the unanimity and the sacrifice with which we fought the war, the senator said,

> let us, with equal zeal, equal candor and equal purpose, consider – not as sentimentalists but as 'realists' – the calculated risks to us if we turn our backs upon our foreign friends and let them sink for want of aid which might have kept them alive and free.
>
> I quote the quiet but impressive eloquence of Ambassador Douglas[6] speaking a few days ago before our committee:
> 'it is almost a certainly that if we do nothing, such chaos, disorder and confusion will exist that men's minds will take hold of queer ideas hostile to their own traditions and inimical to ours. In a western world the consequences to us can be profound. The costs to us may be expressed in an incalculable number of billions of dollars. It may be expressed in impairments of our own historic free institutions. So it seems to me that our vital national interests are deeply concerned.'[7]

We have no choice – but certainly we can improve on the techniques we have followed over the past two and a half years.

Then there are the pessimists who, while admitting the consequences of inaction, insist that Europe is doomed anyway and that it has had its day. America, they say, with its approximately 140 million people cannot save the 270 million people of Western Europe, not to speak of the 450 million people of China. Meanwhile, they point out, we have world-wide commitments, and we should go slow in Europe and not put too many eggs in one basket.

If the people of Europe themselves adopted this fatalistic attitude, there would be justice in this viewpoint. But they do not. They have not abandoned the fight. It is all too easy for us, with the protection of thousands of miles of ocean, the possession of the atom bomb, with industry and agricultural production at new highs, and with a vigorous, healthy, well-fed population, to draw invidious comparisons with what is happening in Europe. But I wish to record here that it took no little courage for the sixteen nations of Western Europe, many of them within easy range of guided missiles from territories under Soviet control, to stand up and say, in the face of Soviet menaces, that they proposed to work

6. Republican Lewis W. Douglas had been financial advisor to Lucius D. Clay, American military governor for Germany. In February 1947, he was made ambassador to Great Britain.
7. The text of Vandenberg's speech is reprinted in *New York Times*, 25 November 1947, 14.

with the United States of America to save their institutions; to work not along communistic, but along democratic lines. This does not indicate that the people of Europe have given up. And as long as they maintain their determination, there is hope and comfort in the situation.

No doubt there are soft spots. The people of Europe have been, for the most part, undernourished for seven long years. This applies particularly to the industrial workers and the city dwellers, and it is here that one looks for the industrial production so necessary to recovery. But even in the field of industry [there] are hopeful signs.

For those who claim the British won't work, it is interesting to note that in the last weeks of 1947 coal production in England reached the highest point since 1942. On December 17 the British announced that in 1948 they would be able to increase their exports of coal by some 80 thousand tons per week, which would mean an increase in 1948 to 10 million tons, or 4 million tons over the amount the British undertook to send abroad as part of its contribution to the Marshall Plan. In announcing the increased exports in the House of Commons, the minister of fuel and power stated that British coal exports would go primarily to nations which aim to cooperate in the Marshall Plan.

In France, Italy, and elsewhere in Western Europe there are optimistic signs in a picture that we must recognize to be desperately difficult as long as Germany remains an industrial vacuum. But a little cheer is even coming from the Ruhr, where coal production has been steadily increasing.

Let us not forget that there is no position in Europe to gloss over the difficulties. The streets of London are placarded with this sign: "We are up against it. We work or want." As long as Europe has the will to work there is a chance for recovery. I am confident there is this will to work where there are the tools with which to work. This means food and fuel as well as raw materials and machinery; and finally, *hope*.

Those who write off Western Europe have a further argument, and it is a potent one. They say Europe, cut in two by the Iron Curtain is strangled, or, to use another metaphor, is like an individual whose jugular vein has been cut. The highly populated industrial West, these critics say, cut off from its natural markets and sources of raw materials and foods in the East, cannot survive.

Undoubtedly, the difficulties of Western Europe are vastly accentuated by the Iron Curtain, but, as of today at least, there is a tendency to exaggerate the economic consequences of the political division between East and West. Let us take some examples. At the end of 1947, the trade of Poland, for instance, was as much with the West across the Iron Curtain as it was with the East. That of Czechoslovakia was predominantly with the West. Trade agreements were being made between our zones of Germany and many of the countries behind the Iron Curtain. Britain had just concluded a trade agreement with Russia under which, in return for machinery and equipment, she was promised 800 thousand tons of coarse grains. The tendency of trade to flow along natural lines is very strong.

And Russia, too, has her own difficulties. She can neither supply the needs of her satellite countries nor can she usefully consume the goods which they produce. These satellite countries have largely the same type of economy as Russia. Most of them are still predominantly agricultural. Under normal conditions they have food surpluses and their industrial needs can only be met in the West. Western Europe would normally have an industrial surplus and agricultural needs. Short of actual military occupation, Communist Russia will have great difficulty in holding her satellites if this means that they must drop all trade and commercial intercourse with the West. All that Soviet diplomacy has risked so far is to try to direct a greater share of this trade eastward. Natural economic trends defy the dictates of politics.

There are also critics of the Marshall Plan who tell us that it is futile to give aid while many of the countries of Europe, in addition to maintaining unbalanced budgets and inflated currencies, indulge in socialistic experimentation and nationalize their industries. Aid under these conditions, the critics say, is both dangerous and futile – dangerous because we would, in effect, be helping to build up an alien type of life and one hostile to our own institutions; futile because this socialistic experimentation is economically unsound and makes recovery impossible. These critics suggest that no country should "qualify" for our aid unless it agrees to abandon socialistic practices.

These arguments are subtle and appeal to the individualistic spirit of America. Certainly our ability to help Europe will be lessened if we start out with divided councils on this important issue. But here, it seems to me, there are certain basic principles on which agreement can be reached.

Firstly, here in this country, by and large, we do not believe that either general welfare or efficiency are promoted by socializing or nationalizing industry. We have come to recognize, however, that with the complications of our modern life a measure of state influence and control, particularly in the field of public utilities, is inevitable. We must therefore recognize that the question of state interference or supervision in business matters is a question of degree rather than of principle. All that we can say is that we do not like to see it unduly extended here, and we do not wish to encourage the far more drastic tendencies towards nationalization in other countries.

Secondly, the tendency toward state socialism arises out of abnormal economic conditions and can best be met by the restoration of healthy economic conditions. Conditions of economic dislocation, of shortages of foods and raw materials, tend to force the individual and industry into the arms of government. As normal conditions return, this trend is likely to be reversed.

Thirdly, there is, as far as I know, only one certain rule in international relations. This rule is that any interference by one country in the internal affairs of another creates resentment and is sure to produce a result exactly the opposite of the one intended. We have recently had a rather sad experience in trying to tell another country what sort of a government it should have. Let us not repeat the error.

Fourthly, if Western Europe is to be saved and if we are to meet the basic challenge which communism has presented to us, we need friends and allies. We must find them among those peoples who believe with us in the fundamentals of human liberty, even though they apply those principles somewhat differently than we. As Governor Dewey stated in his speech on November 5, 1947, "There are two worlds today. This is enough. In fact, it is one too many."[8] We should not erect barriers and create a third world, namely, one in which there are those who, at the moment, believe and practice a measure of state socialism.

It is quite true, however, that the trend toward state socialism presents another type of challenge to us, and one which we can and should meet. And if we meet it we will have resolved our problem. Without preaching or dictating, we can continue to show – and we do not need to say a word about it – that the free enterprise system is the most efficient and productive system in the world. It has proved this in its mobilization to win a great war and in its quick reconversion to the ways of peace. It is proving it again in the preparation which it is now making to consolidate the peace

8. *New York Times*, 6 November 1947, 12.

by providing not only for its own needs but also by making the most generous grants of aid to other countries that have ever been known in time of peace. This object lesson, together with the effect of a gradual improvement in economic conditions in Europe, will help to turn the tide in favor of the system of free enterprise. It will do more than any steps we could take to try to force any socialist countries of Western Europe into our pattern by threatening to withhold our aid.

Other critics warn us that dollars will not save the world. Henry Hazlitt, in his widely publicized booklet *Will Dollars Save The World[?]* (The Foundation for Economic Education, Inc., 1947),[9] suggests that we cannot feed the world, that Europe has great unused resources and that our help will be of little value unless Europe "discontinues policies which unbalance its trade and discourage or prevent production." Another difficulty, he finds, is that "there is no scientific...way of measuring either Europe's 'needs' for aid or our 'available resources' for supplying it," – which is very much as though a physician said to his patient that because he could not fully diagnose his illness he would refuse to treat him.[10]

Inflation, intergovernmental borrowing, economic autarchy, and New Dealism generally are condemned by Mr. Hazlitt, who has pictured Western Europe as a conglomeration of states revelling in foolish fiscal policies and refusing to take any measures for their own recovery.

Mr. Hazlitt has adopted a method of argumentation which is quite subtle and which has impressed a great many people. He has put alongside the Marshall Plan a kind of a straw man, which he has endowed with certain characteristics, and then he has proceeded to demolish this straw man and thereby creates the impression that he has simultaneously demolished the Marshall Plan. Here is an example of this type of argument.

We cannot feed the whole world, he says, as we produce only 12 percent of the world's food supply. Certainly no one would quarrel with this, but no one has made any such preposterous suggestion. According to the statistics, there are some 2.1 billion people in the world. Should that fact preclude us from giving aid to the 85 million people of France and Italy who face critical food shortages because of a crop failure? It seems a complete *non sequitur*. It is more instructive to see what, as a practical matter,

9. Published on 29 October 1947.
10. Hazlitt, *Will Dollars Save the World?*, 85, 86.

we can do if our interests dictate. In 1947, with a bumper crop, we had an exportable surplus of some 500 million bushels of grain. This we were able to send and sell abroad without substantially affecting the diet of the American citizen. On the basis of a minimum of say 200[0] calories per day, this would keep between 65 and 70 million people alive for one year, assuming an all-wheat diet. Of course, our grain, which went to many countries, supplemented the diet of several times that number of people. This was the measure of our capabilities in 1947, the year of the greatest wheat crop in our history. 1947 shipments are not likely to be equalled in future years, and our present acreage and grain, we are told, is well in excess of what is desirable for the long-term maintenance of production and for the conservation of our agricultural resources. What we will do in future years as regards food shipments abroad will depend not one whit on the total world population. It will depend upon resources available for export, available foreign purchasers, and the amount of aid which we shall give in support of our overall foreign policy.

We can quite accept the general tenor of Mr. Hazlitt's suggestions that unsound fiscal and economic policies can make any outside help futile, and he leaves us to conclude that such is the case of the West European countries. Here we think that Mr. Hazlitt is at least partly in error. Certainly many mistakes have been made, and not only in the democratic countries of Europe but in the United States since the end of the war. But there seems now to be on both sides of the water a tendency to recognize these mistakes and to take measures to restore a more healthy economy. In Europe little Belgium has led the way. Recently Italy has courageously devalued its currency and pulled in its belt. Both France and Britain, under austerity regimes, are adopting austerity measures.

Here, for example, is what Britain has done, as told us by Don Cook, New York *Herald Tribune*, December 22. "With a solid month of coal production in excess of four million tons weekly...Great Britain at last appears to have turned the corner.... November [1947] was a remarkable month and there is now every evidence that a downward economic cycle has at last been checked.... November steel production was maintained at the highest levels in British history....The cotton industry...attained the highest production level since 1941. In many secondary categories – bicycles, commercial vehicles, clocks, chemicals, tractors, agricultural implements – Britain is producing more than she ever produced in her history and in some cases, such as tractors, nearly seven times as much as ever before."[11] Real progress has been made in Europe. And while the methods employed will not always satisfy the old-line conservatives, this does not mean that a free world has gone.

One of Mr. Hazlitt's chief points of attack is intergovernmental lending, and he has here the really unfortunate experience with the British loan of 1946 to bolster his view. He seems to overlook the fact, however, that it was never contemplated that intergovernmental loans should have substantial place in the Marshall Plan. Certainly we can quite agree that we don't need to give away our money or our goods to aid production and employment here at home. One may ask, however, what would happen if we continued to have a wheat surplus, as in 1947, if foreign markets were closed.

We cannot count on gratitude, Mr. Hazlitt suggests, and we cannot purchase good will. If anyone favors the Marshall Plan on the ground that we are doing it solely for good will purposes, he should reconsider his position. If it is not justified on the grounds of American security we should not embark upon it, but security presumes that other countries have some element of good will toward the United States.

Mr. Hazlitt's booklet is not really an attack on the Marshall Plan as it is evolving. It is an attack on a different and largely nonexistent program. The Europe which he describes is a very different place than the Europe which is facing up to its problems today.

Like so many who are excellent as destructive critics, Mr. Hazlitt seems to me to be rather shy of ideas as to the elements of a constructive program. His panacea for dealing with communism is to expound the merits of the free enterprise system as contrasted with the hunger, terror, and slavery under communism. The difficulty here is that you can hardly impress the desperate and hungry people of Western Europe with the virtues of a complacent capitalism by merely talking to them about it. You can only build such people into a society that can resist the inroads of communism if they have food and the tools with which to work. Kenneth Galbraith,[12] in his review of Mr. Hazlitt's booklet, *New York Times*, December 21, 1947, has well expressed how Europe might react. "How would a cold, supperless family in Paris

11. Don Cook, "Britain Climbing Toward Recovery," New York *Herald Tribune*, 22 December 1947, 22.

12. John Kenneth Galbraith, before World War II teaching Economics at Harvard and Princeton, had been Director of Economic Security Policy of the Department of State in 1946. At the end of 1946, he worked for *Fortune*. He had written *Recovery in Europe* (Washington, D.C., 1946).

respond to a lush radio description of American white bread, steaks and oil burners and an elucidation of the system that provides them – all this, mind you, as a substitute for more tangible aid? I should think it would be just the thing to cause Jean to grab his scarf and beret and go and join the nearest riot."[13]

Senator Taft[14] has added one point of criticism which deserves respectful attention. He objects to what he calls "the balance of payment approach." In effect, what the State Department has been doing, he says, has been to say to those countries (the sixteen European powers) "'Figure out everything you want to import, and what you can export. We will criticize your figures to some extent, and perhaps scale them down a little, but we will advance you the difference.' That is the so-called balance-of-payments theory." Senator Taft goes on to say,

> the whole idea that we are to make good the deficit in the export-import balance of every country in the world is a completely fallacious idea and one which will completely wreck the United States if we go through with it…. [I]t seems to me that all we can do in each case is to say to these countries, 'How much wheat do you need? We have so much wheat….' And make a deal with them on a certain number of bushels, and we will finance certain other things. Let them make their own balance after that…. We should determine the things which we are willing to ship and confine them to the things which we think would help those countries to go to work, rather than simply to solve the financial difficulties of every government.[15]

The *New York Times*, November 30, 1947, in commenting on the Senator's speech points out that what the Marshall Plan proposes to do is not to give the European countries what they want to import but to make up the difference between what Europe can now export and "what it must import to keep a democratic civilization alive." The *Times* goes on to say,

> The result of the Taft Plan, if it can be called that, would be to abolish the ERP and to reduce European aid to a disjointed series of retail operations. If the British loan and the UNRRA gifts were errors, as Senator Taft believes, it would repeat those errors all over the map. We would not be saving money – we would be throwing it down the drain. And we would not be saving Europe – or ourselves.[16]

13. *New York Times*, 21 December 1947, sec. VII, 6, 14. The citation is from ibid., 14.

14. Senator Robert A. Taft was leading the conservative opposition to the Marshall Plan.

15. Taft made this speech in the Senate on 28 November 1947. The text is reprinted in the *New York Times*, 29 November 1947, 4.

16. *New York Times*, 30 November 1947, sec. IV, 10.

The Marshall Plan cannot fill the gap between the European exports and European imports. Its purpose should be to supply some of the food and materials needed to start in motion forces which will narrow that gap and eventually eliminate it. The gap is only an evidence of the magnitude of Europe's need, not necessarily an indication of what we can give.

Another criticism of the Marshall Plan is that a mistake has been made in not proposing that it be carried out through the United Nations. Some of these critics and skeptics are those who are fronting for the isolationists and who wish to see the Plan fail anyway. Others are quite sincere, believing, in general, that all great international projects should be funnelled as far as possible through the United Nations. The latter point to UNRRA as an example of the possibility of an international program of aid. Undoubtedly, many people were honestly disturbed when the Truman Doctrine was promulgated without reference to the United Nations.

These critics deserve a forthright answer. The Marshall Plan cannot be carried out through the United Nations because Russia and her satellites have vetoed it. If today our aid were funnelled through the United Nations, it would mean, in effect, that while we, the United States, are putting up the money or supplying the goods necessary to carry out the plan, we would be faced with crippling vetoes and obstacles at every turn by Russia and her satellites, who have openly proclaimed their intention of sabotaging any general plan for European recovery and have refused to participate in it. Russia has made it impossible to use the United Nations as the vehicle for giving effect to the Marshall Plan.

This does not mean that the various organizations of the United Nations cannot and should not be used in a consultative or other capacity to the extent that this is possible in the light of the Russian attitude. For example, the United Nations has set up an Economic Committee for Europe (ECE) primarily devoted to the study of European needs. This organization has held two sessions in Geneva in 1947. Its membership includes certain western powers and the USSR, Byelo-Russia and the Ukraine and, in addition, Yugoslavia, Poland, and Czechoslovakia. When these countries sit down to discuss the general economic reorganization of Europe with their colleagues from the West, including England, France, Belgium, the Lowlands, the Scandinavian countries, Turkey, and Greece, they run head on into the objections which Molotov raised at the Paris conference.

However, this committee can perform useful work in keeping up economic contact across the Iron Curtain. Through its subsidiary organizations, particularly the European Coal Organization (ECO) it can help in the allocation of coal and possibly facilitate an exchange of Silesian coal against machinery needed by Poland. It can seek an economic bridge between East and West.

Our policy here should be clear cut. Use the United Nations wherever possible; keep it advised of all action taken to give effect to the Marshall Plan, and seek every opportunity through its facilities to break down economic barriers.

Frank Gannett[17] and the press and news service which he controls has voiced the line of criticism which appeals most strongly to our primitive and selfish instincts. "Our first job," he said, "is to make America so powerful in every way that no one will attack us. Pouring billions into Europe will lower our standard of living, increase our tax burdens, raise prices to heights never reached before, and make it impossible to build a sure defense against any foe."

Any expenditure under the Marshall Plan will constitute a tax burden, and it may have some influence on prices, although here the experts differ sharply. But when Mr. Gannett says that the cheapest way to build up our defense is by withholding aid from Europe and putting it into armaments he is entering onto very debatable ground. If Europe and Asia succumb to communism and the United States stands practically alone, we will find that the amount we will then have to spend for armaments will make the proposed outlays for European aid seem only a drop in the bucket. If the advance of communism is peacefully checked in Europe and the democracies of the West are supported, we will have made an investment in security on a far more economical basis than by following Mr. Gannett's suggestion of an armed isolation.

The issues are shaping up today much as they did in 1919–1920, and then twenty years after that in 1939–1940. Shall we retire into isolation, arm ourselves to the teeth, and wait and see what happens? Or shall we make a determined effort to help those nations, whose views concord with ours, in opposing the advance of communism? It is right and proper that there should be a thorough debate on this issue, which is fundamental to the Marshall Plan.

---

17. Frank E. Gannett was a millionaire newspaper publisher who owned a chain of daily newspapers in small and medium-sized cities, mostly in the state of New York.

CHAPTER 7

Man Cannot Live by Bread Alone

Critics of the Marshall Plan, as we have seen, claim that dollars will not save Europe. There is an element of truth in this, but not quite in the way the critics mean it. Certainly I would agree that we cannot buy security against the onward march of communism by a mere outpouring of dollars or of goods. Nor can we effectively protect ourselves by posting any thin line of armed guards around the vast periphery of Russia. To contain the aggressive Communist movement, we need not only material strength, we also need a spiritual force. We need a force which will grip men's minds, not merely provide for their bodies or for their physical protection.

Communism moves into soft spots; not only the spots which are soft economically but into those spots which are soft spiritually. So far, communism has never peacefully gained control in any great area which had previously known liberty as we understand it. In Russia the people merely turned from one dictatorship to another. In certain of the Balkan countries which today are minions of Russia the ideals of human liberty were only skin-deep, and elsewhere in satellite countries the Communist indoctrination was preceded by military occupation and administered with force.

But we would be deluding ourselves if we did not recognize that in various countries of the world of today the Communists made real progress in the immediate postwar days, even though they have fallen short of achieving control. The idea of a paternalistic and all-controlling government made serious inroads among the hungry and dispirited peoples who emerged in 1945 from years of war. This has taken place largely because distraught men and women were searching for some way out, and communism, with its easy answer, was not vigorously met by a spiritual force which brought out the values of human liberty as contrasted with the degradation of human slavery.

In this respect, the end of the war in 1945 was quite different from the war end in 1918. Thirty years ago, as the first world war ceased, there was a note of high optimism and resolve. Despite the great human and material loses, Woodrow Wilson succeeded in capturing the imagination of the postwar world. People were to be freed and helped to build a future on the basis of liberty and self-determination. The League of Nations was to insure future peace. People in Europe went about the task of reconstruction with hope. The momentum this gave led to rapid world recovery in the 1920s.

Unfortunately, the international idealism of those days was not coupled with economic realism. Political self-determination did not prevent economic nationalism. In fact, it seemed to foster it. The United States withdrew and left a Europe far weaker than we realized to shift for itself politically. The gains of the twenties were lost in the thirties.

In the period following V-E and V-J Days in 1945, there seemed to be spiritual force in the democratic world to match the militant aggressiveness and subtle propaganda of the Soviets. The United Nations, it is true, had been launched, but its birth was beclouded by conflicts between East and West, between the veto and free discussion.

As a result, the West European powers in the postwar period began to fear that they were likely to become pawns in a conflict between Russia and the United States, both in and out of the United Nations. Many, particularly in Europe, accustomed to the play of power politics, interpreted what was happening as merely another struggle for world mastery between the two most powerful countries of the globe. The real issues did not at first emerge, namely, that the struggle was not one of power but one of principle – that it was a struggle between the principles which underlie the Magna Carta, the Declaration of Independence, the French and the American Revolutions, on the one hand, and the materialism of Marx, Lenin, and Stalin, on the other – a struggle between the rights of the individual and the claims of an all-powerful materialistic state.

It is only as we enter the year 1948 that these issues are slowly being clarified. The people of Western Europe are now beginning to gain perspective as to what is at stake.

Two years or more of broadsides and propaganda from Moscow, together with the tirades of Molotov and Vishinsky[1] at

---

1. Andrei Y. Vishinsky, chief prosecutor during the Great Purge trials in Moscow in the 1930s, served as deputy Soviet foreign minister. He was known for his bitter verbal attacks against the United States and became foreign minister in 1949.

the United Nations and in the meetings of the Council of Foreign Ministers, have not convinced any part of the free world that America is either militaristic or war minded. But past failures of this propaganda have only led Russia to redouble it in virulence and mendacity. The only converts they have made by this propaganda have been behind the Iron Curtain.

It is evidence of real progress that the United States has dulled the edge of this propaganda weapon and has won the respect and confidence – confidence in our objectives and our motives – of the governments in London, Paris, Rome, and elsewhere in Western Europe. But we need also to become the apostles of a peaceful offensive against the advance of Marxist materialism. There must be a Marshall Plan of the spirit as well as a plan to feed and clothe and give warmth and work. As Mr. Hamilton Fish Armstrong[2] well puts it in *The Calculated Risk* (Macmillan Company, 1947), we want Europe to know not only that we can give them what Russia cannot, namely, material help, but also "we offer what Soviet Russia will not – political freedom."

> We want to help the people of Europe to escape, in our interest and theirs, from the isolation of misery, confusion and apprehension in which they have been living. We want to carry them word that we still care about them as we did when we landed on the Channel beaches. We want them to know that we hold hard to the same course we set when we put our signature to the Charter of the United Nations. We want them to understand that our system of democratic government and private enterprise is living and growing, adapting itself to the needs of the present as it did to those of the past. We want them to remain part of the civilization of which they were so largely the originator and so long the center. We want them, in this sense, to be with us.[3]

The task of leadership has been thrust upon us and we should not deceive ourselves with the thought that we can meet the responsibilities of this position by appropriations of money alone.

At the outset I suggested that the old Europe is gone and that it is not the purpose of any Marshall Plan to try to recreate it. Secretary Marshall, in his report on the London conference [of the Council of Foreign Ministers], December [19], 1947, put it this way: "In the war struggle, Europe was in a large measure shat-

---

2. Hamilton F. Armstrong was the editor of the Council on Foreign Relations's quarterly *Foreign Affairs* and, together with Dulles, had taken part in the Council's War and Peace Studies program and a number of council study and discussion groups after 1945.

3. Hamilton F. Armstrong, *The Calculated Risk* (New York, 1947) 15.

tered. As a result, a political vacuum was created and until this vacuum has been filled by the restoration of a healthy European community, it does not appear possible that paper agreements can assure a lasting peace."[4]

Europe today is particularly vulnerable to communism. A void has been created and into this void there must go not only economic help but ideas and a spiritual force. Europe has shown that it is ready to respond. The countries of Western Europe have met the stress and strain of the past two years without taking the easy way by recourse to dictatorship. This is a hopeful sign, as is the fact that in their courageous stand against the recent Communist attempt to sabotage their economies, France and Italy adhered strictly to democratic processes.

But it is not enough that the countries in Western Europe should show individual strength. Separately they will not be strong enough, even with American aid, to work out a livable future. In his life of Benjamin Franklin, Carl Van Doren describes the signing of the American Declaration of Independence. As John Hancock, presiding officer, signed first in bold letters, he is reported to have remarked, "We must be unanimous; there must be no pulling different ways; we must all hang together." At this point, as legend tells it, Franklin added, "We must indeed all hang together, or most assuredly we shall all hang separately." That is the position of Europe today.[5]

The principles underlying the Declaration of Independence became common to the United States and to much of Western Europe. But the idea of unity was relatively much easier to establish in a new continent in the face of external peril than in a Europe with its encrusted traditions. Today, as Western Europe faces its common peril, there is an opportunity as never before to make progress toward that goal of unity.

The problem is an infinitely complex one and will have to be worked out largely by the European powers themselves. But if we underwrite a Marshall Plan, we have a large stake in the results. The United States is the only country outside of Europe which can really help to bring the European states together in a union which will be a defensive bulwark against the advance of communism. The idea of a European economic union, a United States of Europe, is not a project of mere dreamers. It has the serious backing of leaders in all countries of Europe. It is generally recognized

4. A transcript of the radio broadcast is reprinted in *New York Times*, 20 December 1947, 4.
5. Carl van Doren, *Benjamin Franklin* (New York, 1938) reprinted 1973.

as a necessary step, but too many people throw up their hands and say that the practical obstacles are too great.

Europe cannot do it alone. Nor can America impose its political or economic views on Europe. We can help to show that only such a unity will give driving force to the ideals of protecting human liberty. It is only thus that our aid can be effective.

A start has been made. It was made when the sixteen West European powers met in Paris. They recognized that closer unity was necessary. They met together as Europeans; they talked about European, not national, recovery; they laid plans for practical steps to effect a customs union; they discussed a series of projects for the common exploitation of new sources for electrical power, pooling agreements in the field of transportation, and other means of mutual help between the participating countries. They announced "that the prosperity of each of them depends upon the restoration of the prosperity of all." This could "best be achieved by sustained common efforts," and the CEEC report included this solemn assurance: that if means for carrying out the program were made available, the sixteen states would be ready to set up an organization to insure to the "full extent possible by joint action, the realization of the economic conditions necessary to enable the general objectives to which each country has pledged itself to be effectively achieved." Here are the seeds from which European unity might grow.[6]

It is all too easy to let lapse this truly epochal step forward in the direction of economic and eventually political unity. Each of the countries may desire to negotiate with us separately, hoping thereby to get a more ample share under any Marshall Plan. This could only lead to economic rivalries and deepen nationalism. The United States has here an entirely legitimate basis for inducing these European countries to act together so that our aid would serve to break down and not to build up barriers. We can rightly insist on this because unless we succeed here we may fail of our ultimate objective of bringing about European recovery. This idea of a European goal, a European drive to restore and preserve not only a reasonable standard of economic life but a basis for real European freedom, can give an overall spiritual impetus to any recovery plan. It can bring to Europeans a faith in a better future.

Finally, American aid to Europe is not solely a matter for government dealing. It is here that we have a great advantage over Russia, where only the state can act. The outpouring of private

6. Department of State, *Committee of European Co-operation: Volume I*, 2, 40.

American philanthropy, the interest taken by individuals on this side of the water in the relief of the distress of those in Europe, has had a far-reaching effect. Dunkirk, New York, adopted Dunkerque, France, and a bond was built up between those two cities which is unique in history. The example has been contagious, and we will see the citizens of many towns and cities in the United States following this example and bringing to a troubled world the element of individual interest, individual help, and the type of sharing which is at the basis of Christian teachings. It is the outpouring of aid from a free people to those who are struggling to remain free.

We are apt to underrate or overlook the importance of the psychological factors in a recovery program. Don Cook, in an article on Britain in the New York *Herald Tribune* of December 22, 1947, to which I have referred, remarks that the wedding of the Princess Elizabeth had a galvanizing effect on the imaginations of the British people. All of a sudden, they seemed to produce more coal and turn their freight cars around more quickly. "At perhaps the very moment when the country was scraping the bottom...the royal wedding swelled every heart with memories of the glorious British past and instilled confidence in the future." People are still human beings, and very human, at that.[7]

The other day there was a brief story in *The New York Times* (December 21, 1947) by Mallory Browne. In simple language he recounted what happened in Paris when the Friendship Train with the free will offering of the American people arrived in the French capital.[8] Here is how he told it.

> A Christmas story came true today for the school children of Paris. They saw with their own eyes dozens and dozens of big trucks drive up filled with gifts of food for them from the Friendship Train.
>
> I wish you could have seen them – all you school children back home everywhere in the United States. Their big eyes shone and their little dirty faces glowed under their black school berets or their pigtails tied up with ribbons.
>
> I wish you could have heard them, too, when those trucks drove up

7. Don Cook, "Britain Climbing Toward Recovery," New York *Herald Tribune*, 22 December 1947, 22.

8. The Friendship Food Train was conceived by Washington columnist Drew Pearson and sponsored by a national committee headed by motion picture producer Harry Warner. It started out in Hollywood, CA, on 12 November 1947 with twelve freight cars. When it reached New York City, about 270 cars of food had been donated to be sent to communities in France and Italy. Drew Pearson, the pen name of Andrew Russell Pearson, was one of the most influential and controversial newspaper journalists in the United States.

onto the Place de l'Hotel de Ville all decorated with French and American flags and big posters in French saying: 'To Our French Friends From the Bottom of Our Hearts.' How they cheered and shouted! How they waved their little French and American flags!

There were thousands of them. I don't suppose all the children of Paris were there, but it looked like it and sounded like it. They cheered and cheered until I thought it sounded like a shrill surf rising and falling but never stopping. What a racket they made. It reminded me of you back home.

It reminded me of you, too, the way they didn't listen very much to the speeches there on the steps of the City Hall. They were too busy punching and pushing and tickling each other and pulling pigtails and snatching off caps. But they enjoyed themselves even if it was rainy and a heavy mist almost hid the nearby twin towers of Notre Dame de Paris.

They listened, though, when Pierre de Gaulle, the Mayor (yes, he's the brother of General de Gaulle), boomed into the microphone: 'I am going to tell you a beautiful Christmas story.'

I wish you could have heard them exclaim, with one breath: 'Aaahhh.'

And why shouldn't he tell them a Christmas story? The 'Nuit de Noel' was only a few days off. And there, on the banks of the River Seine, propped up against the little bookstalls that line the quais, they could see hundreds and hundreds of Christmas trees from the big flower market near by.

So they listened to M. de Gaulle, and he told them the story of how there was once a man who had an idea about a train to take food to the hungry peoples of Europe.

And there he was, that man, Drew Pearson, standing on the steps. He made a speech, too.

There was a big train that traveled all across the United States, M. de Gaulle said, and he told how you children in the United States brought your own school lunches or the money for them and your own clothes and put them on the train for the children of France. And at the end, just like at the end of a real story, he asked them to tell the American Ambassador and the other Americans who were there what they thought of this Christmas story that they had heard.

Then they cheered and shouted some more and the movie camera men and photographers flashed so many flashlight bulbs it seemed like fireworks in the dull gray evening mist.

Then the band played The Star-Spangled Banner (with a queer sort of French accent) and The Marseillaise. I wish you could have heard that, too.

That was all. At least there was more to the official ceremony inside, but that was all of the Christmas story because the children left then and so did I.

There was something else, though. I wish you could have seen the first Friendship Train from Havre steaming into the Gare St. Lazare in Paris earlier this morning, all decorated with French and American flags, with a band playing and flares burning in the fog.

There were lots of children there, too, and some of them looked a little hungry and somehow I felt especially glad that that train had brought them a little more food and I knew you would be, too, that you all had helped send it to them.

So as some of the French children shouted this afternoon: 'Merci et Joyeux Noel aux Americains.'[9]

I have given Mallory Browne's story just as he wrote it because it shows how a free democratic people can do things which possibly do not cost a vast amount in dollars but which, if they are repeated and kept up and done in different ways as well, can help to change the course of history. Freedom and liberty cannot be preserved by bread alone. But they can be preserved if we can build up a spirit of unity and cooperation among the freedom-loving peoples of Europe and between them and the people of the United States.

9. *New York Times*, 21 December 1947, 1, 21.

CHAPTER 8

The Marshall Plan and Foreign Policy

The Marshall Plan is often described as a scheme to help peoples who are starving and to build up the economies of certain countries with which, over the years, we have had close cultural and economic ties. This view does not put the Plan into its true focus. It is not a philanthropic enterprise. It is far more than that.

The American people have had a long tradition of generosity in meeting distress and disaster abroad. We have done this with little regard for the degree of affection we might have for the particular peoples concerned or its relation to our foreign policy. Thus, on humanitarian grounds we were quick to respond to starvation in Soviet Russia in 1921–22, at a time when we refused to maintain diplomatic relations with that country. We went all out to the aid of Japan after the great earthquake in 1923.

The present program of relief and reconstruction of Europe, which may engage our efforts and our resources over a considerable period of time, is not this sort of an undertaking. It is an integral part of American policy. It is based on our view of the requirements of American security and is a logical development of the trends of our foreign policy over more than a century. If we are not to depart from the course of that policy we have little choice but to proceed vigorously with the Marshall Plan, even though we recognize that the results are not clearly predictable today, as no one can say with assurance that even the great resources which America can safely make available for export to others will be adequate to turn the tide of economic disintegration in Europe. But as we see it today this is the only peaceful course now open to us which may answer the communist challenge to our way of life and our national security.

In his great "Study of History," Professor Toynbee has suggested that the test of national survival depends largely upon the interplay of forces which he calls "challenge" and "response." As long as a civilization can meet the challenge directed against it, it prevails; if the challenge is bitter and still the people grapple successfully with it, then a great and strong civilization results. If, however, peoples go along without meeting any serious resistance they become weak, an easy prey to almost any challenge. And the strongest civilization goes down when it becomes incapable of making an effective response.[1]

A foreign policy is one of the weapons with which a state deals with the challenges which face it. If a country is small, with modest resources, its policy must be directed to reducing the area of challenge. Switzerland is an example. When, by geography of circumstances, a country has worldwide interests and responsibilities, it must either provide the resources to meet these responsibilities or attempt to reduce its commitments. Britain today is doing the latter. The United States is clearly embarking on the former course.

All states, whether the most powerful and aggressive or the most peacefully minded, would define the objectives of foreign policy in much the same way, namely, "to protect vital interests." If a country conceives that its vital interests are to gain "a place in the sun" or to enlarge its "Lebensraum," to take the slogans of Germany in World War I and [World War] II, then foreign policy becomes dynamic and aggressive. If, as in the case of Germany, there are inadequate resources to back up such a policy, the result is disaster.

On the other hand, if the objective of a foreign policy is merely to preserve an acquired and recognized position, the protection of vital interests may be achieved quite modestly as long as we have a well-ordered, international society. Unfortunately, today nothing is well ordered, and there is no easy way to achieve security. National frontiers are not always the safe defensive frontiers. The United States – a satisfied and peacefully minded state – is faced with a desperately urgent and difficult task in trying to insure that the countries which occupy strategically important positions on the flanks of our national frontiers are safe and trustworthy friends.

Viewed in this light, American foreign policy today is seeking the very same objectives as when we proposed the Monroe

---

1. Arnold J. Toynbee, *A Study of History* (New York, 1935–1961) 12 volumes.

Doctrine or developed the principles of the Open Door in the Far East. There is a common motif which runs through it all: the desire to insure not only our geographical integrity but also the paths of possible access to our national frontiers. We often forget that the Monroe Doctrine was occasioned almost as much by Russian claims to the northwest coast of North America as it was by designs of European potentates on South America.

Looking back, historically, our first major objective in foreign policy was to get Europe out of the North American continent so as to have no unpleasantly strong neighbors right here in our midst. Thanks to the inadvertent help of Napoleon and the concentration of the nations of Europe on their own problems, we had largely achieved this by 1823, the date of the Monroe Doctrine. The one great exception was Canada, and here statesmanship on both sides of the water helped to create a great, friendly, and independent northern neighbor by evolution rather than by revolution or attempted conquest. Here we had a safe frontier.

The second great objective was to get and keep Europe out of this hemisphere; hence the Monroe Doctrine, and later the war with Spain. Fortunately, the Anglo-Saxons are a practical-minded people, and when the basic objective was achieved, we never worried much over small exceptions, such as foreign possessions in the Caribbean and the Guianas, and, although we generally forget it, we did not even object to two infringements of the Monroe Doctrine even after it was promulgated, namely, the British acquisitions of British Honduras and the Falklands.

The Open Door in China was in some respects the counterpart in Asia of the Monroe Doctrine in South America. But here it took a somewhat different turn. The Open Door was not an exclusion act, but a Sherman Anti-Trust Law in foreign relations.[2] We wanted no one to have a monopoly, but everyone to have reasonable equality of opportunity within a framework which protected the integrity and sovereignty of China. It was emphasis on this latter development of the Open Door policy, the insistence on Chinese national integrity, which was the forerunner of the Hull[3] policy, and eventually brought us into conflict with Japan.[4]

2. Sherman Antitrust Act, named after Senator John Sherman, became law on 2 July 1890.

3. Cordell Hull was secretary of state of the Roosevelt administrations from 1933 to 1944.

4. Japanese occupation of Manchuria in 1931 and the installation of a puppet government had already led to a decline in American-Japanese relations. When in 1937 Japanese troops occupied China's main coastal cities and much of the hinterland, relations rapidly deteriorated further.

The basic philosophy back of the Monroe Doctrine – and one which has stood us in good stead for many decades – was that we should stay out of Europe and Europe should stay out of Americas. "Europe has a set of primary interests which to us have none or a very remote relation" and therefore "it must be unwise in us to implicate ourselves by artificial ties in the ordinary vicissitudes of her politics or the ordinary combinations and collisions of her friendships or enmities." These words are taken from Washington's Farewell Address of 1796. Or, to quote from the Monroe Doctrine Declaration itself, "in the wars of the European powers in matters relating to themselves we have never taken any part, nor does it comport with our policy to do so." That statements such as those of Washington, Jefferson, Monroe, and John Quincy Adams could have set forth a policy which held good for almost a century is a tribute to any man or group of men. But these wise framers of our early foreign policy carefully qualified their remarks. Washington said we were not to implicate ourselves by *"artificial ties"* and the *"ordinary vicissitudes"* of European politics, while Monroe referred to the wars of European powers *"in matters relating to themselves."*[5]

As our policy toward Europe developed in the face of two German attempts to conquer the Continent and the British Isles, we found that we were up against issues which did not relate solely to the European powers or constitute merely "ordinary vicissitudes" of European politics. We viewed these developments as direct threats to American security.

Our policy toward Europe was not given a distinctive label, such as "Monroe Doctrine" or "Open Door," although it is a logical extension of both. It was sketched in the Fourteen Points of Wilson and in their somewhat weakened counterpart of the recent war, the Atlantic Charter. It was set forth in the League of Nations, unfortunately repudiated by us but now revived in the United Nations. It was based upon our interest in the existence of free and independent nations, brought together among themselves, and with us and other countries, in a world organization.

In effect, this is another way of saying that one of the basic objectives of American policy, as definite as the Monroe Doctrine or the Open Door, is to prevent the domination of Europe or Asia by any one power, whether that power be called Germany or Russia or Japan. This policy stemmed from the thought that such domination, as the world narrowed in effective size, might easily

5. The emphases are Dulles's.

push beyond Europe or Asia and threaten the Western Hemisphere on both flanks. And thus the doctrines of Monroe and John Quincy Adams, of Theodore Roosevelt and Hay,[6] and of Woodrow Wilson and Franklin Roosevelt, have charted for us a course which has led to the proposals of President Truman and Secretary Marshall.

It is interesting to compare what Monroe said in his message of December 1823 with certain passages of Truman's message in March of 1947. While the immediate subject matter of the latter was Greece and Turkey, the implications were far broader. Addressing himself over a century ago to the ambitions of the European powers, Monroe stated:

> We owe it, therefore, to candor and to the amicable relations existing between the United States and those powers to declare that we should consider any attempt on their part to extend their system to any portion of this hemisphere as dangerous to our peace and safety.... [W]e could not view any interposition for the purpose of oppressing them, or controlling in any other manner their destiny, by any European power in any other light than as the manifestation of an unfriendly disposition toward the United States... It is impossible that the allied powers should extend their political system to any portion of either continent without endangering our peace and happiness; nor can anyone believe that our southern brethren, if left to themselves, would adopt it of their own accord. It is equally impossible, therefore, that we should behold such interposition in any form with indifference.[7]

President Truman, on March [12], 1947, stated:

> I believe that it must be the policy of the United States to support free peoples who are resisting attempted subjugation by armed minorities or by outside pressures.
>
> I believe that we must assist free peoples to work out their own destinies in their own way.
>
> I believe that our help should be primarily through economic and financial aid which is essential to economic stability and orderly political processes.
>
> The world is not static, and the status quo is not sacred. But we cannot allow changes in the status quo in violation of the Charter of the United Nations by such methods as coercion, or by such subterfuges as political infiltration. In helping free and independent nations to

6. John Hay was secretary of state, 1898 to 1901, during the Spanish-American War.

7. For a reprint of President Monroe's message to Congress, 2 December 1823, see Ian Elliot, *James Monroe, 1758–1831: Chronology – Documents – Bibliographical Aids* (Dobbs Ferry, NY, 1969) 58–70. For the phrases cited, see p. 69.

maintain their freedom, the United States will be giving effect to the principles of the Charter of the United Nations.[8]

The essential difference between the policies enunciated by Monroe and Truman was that Monroe limited his declaration to the American Hemisphere. President Truman, in his statement, set no geographical limitations. Its scope was worldwide. Faced with such a declaration of policy, it is natural that those who are responsible for our international relations should carefully review the resources we have to make the policy effective, and see how we should set about to do it.

There is help in historical precedents. The bold step which President Monroe took in 1823 – almost recklessly bold when one considers the relative military weakness of the United States of those days – proved successful because we were assured of the aid of England and the support of its fleet. This backing was ours not out of Britain's love for its former colonies, but because she wished to curb Russia, Spain, and other rivals. But it was a backing which was none the less precious, and with it a policy was inaugurated which, with minor interludes, helped to preserve peace in the world for nearly a century.

In the light of this page of history, we would do well to recognize that no policy as universal as the Truman Doctrine can be carried out by the United States alone. We need friends and allies. Hence it is natural that we should rely, not alone on England as we did in 1823, but on what we hope will become an association of West European nations ready to act with us so that "free and independent nations" can "maintain their freedom."[9]

The Marshall proposal, as initiated, was not directed primarily to carrying out the Truman Doctrine. The latter was motivated principally by the desire to contain Russian expansion wherever it threatened free peoples who were willing to put up a struggle to maintain their freedom. Secretary Marshall's invitation was directed to Russia as much as to Britain or France. It was a call for European cooperation on a broad scale, across any Iron Curtain, to see whether we could work with Russia not whether we must work to contain Russia.

The Russian attitude has changed all this. They have not merely refused their cooperation, they have declared war on cooperation. By Russia's own choice, therefore, the Marshall Plan cannot be

8. Truman's special message to Congress on Greece and Turkey is reprinted in *Harry S. Truman, 1947*, 176–80.
9. Ibid.

today a program for general European economic reconstruction to include Russia. It has become a test as to whether the economic life of Western Europe can be restored and maintained at a level to prevent the encroachment of Russia. It has become a policy to contain the advance of Russia westward in Europe, an advance which would inevitably follow the economic breakdown of the West.

The Monroe Doctrine was a policy of containment with the objective limited to this hemisphere and directed against the auto-cratic powers in Europe. The Open Door, in its development under Hull, was a policy of containment directed against the monopoly of any power in China. The Truman policy is a doctrine of containment directed against the spread of communism by force. We have started to implement this policy in Greece and Turkey, and, if the Marshall Plan is realized, we will be acting in a broader field to contain the advance of communism in Europe.

The feasibility of a policy of containment has been vigorously debated here in the United States. The policy was elaborated in an article on the "Sources of Soviet Conduct" in *Foreign Affairs* in July 1947, an article the authoritative character of which was only tem-porarily protected by the anonymity of the author, Mr. X.[10] After a lucid analysis of Russian policy, the author stated, "It is clear that the main element of any United States policy toward the Soviet Union must be that of a long-term, patient but firm and vigilant containment of Russian expansive tendencies." And he added, "It will be clearly seen that the Soviet pressure against the free insti-tutions of the western world is something that can be contained by the adroit and vigilant application of counterforce at a series of constantly shifting geographical and political points, correspond-ing to the shifts and manœuvres of Soviet policy, but which cannot be charmed or talked out of existence."[11]

Walter Lippmann, in a series of articles, has asserted that even a state as powerful as the United States today could not close the great perimeter of possible Russian aggression. In his opinion, we should work to achieve settlements which would get the Red Army back onto Soviet territory. Peace treaties should be conclud-ed, and we should then build on the ability of the peoples of the world, freed from direct Russian military pressure, to meet the expansionist ideological drive of communism, in the belief and

10. "X" was the pseudonym for George F. Kennan, at that time director of the State Department's Policy Planning Staff.
11. "X" [George F. Kennan], "Sources of Soviet Conduct," *Foreign Affairs* 25 (July 1947): 566–82. For the phrases cited, see pp. 575, 576.

hope that Russia will not take the risk of military aggression. We should contain Russia "by the strategical employment of American power, not by local tactical interventions all around the periphery of the Soviet Union," Lippmann writes.[12]

These rival arguments[13] bring to mind the military dilemma which Germany faced in 1944, and which I observed from an inside post in Switzerland.[14] Knowing that an invasion was coming in France, but not knowing where it would strike, what should be her strategy? There were divided counsels, as the field marshals in command, von Rundstedt,[15] Rommel,[16] and von Kluge,[17] could not agree among themselves or with the German High Command. Should the Germans concentrate their forces along the coast of France and try to repel the invasion at the beachheads? Or should they keep their main force in a mobile reserve, recognizing that the landing could take place, not attempting to meet the Allies on the beaches but, when the point of main attack was discovered, trust in their ability to bring overwhelming forces to bear before our position could be consolidated? The Germans attempted both tactics, and as a result had insufficient forces either on the beaches or in their mobile reserve, to accomplish their objective.

It is, of course, obvious that today we are not equipped to insure an immediate physical, military containment of Russia, and I do not believe that Mr. X's article suggested this. We have only token forces abroad, or possibly they might be better described as forces which are not adequate to contain on land any Russian military move. Further, these forces are in only four crucial areas of

12. *Herald-Tribune*, 15 December 1947, 21, under the title "The Limit of Communist Expansion," in his column "Today and Tomorrow." Earlier that year, Lippmann had used his column to write twelve small essays as a response to Kennan's *Foreign Affairs* article. They appeared between 2 September and 2 October 1947. All twelve articles were published by Harper and Brothers under the title *The Cold War: A Study in U.S. Foreign Policy* (New York, 1947). Together with Kennan's article, this booklet was reprinted in 1972.

13. Kennan later maintained that Lippmann had actually misunderstood many of his arguments and that on most issues he saw eye-to-eye with Lippmann. See Kennan, *Memoirs 1925–1950* (Boston, 1967) 359–61.

14. In 1944 Dulles was head of the Office of Strategic Services (OSS) in Bern, Switzerland.

15. German field marshal Gerd von Rundstedt became commander-in-chief, west, in 1942.

16. Defeated by the British in Africa, Erwin Rommel was put in charge of defending the French coast against an expected Allied invasion in 1944.

17. Günther von Kluge replaced von Rundstedt on 31 July 1944, after von Rundstedt had been unable to stop the Anglo-American advances after the landing in Normandy on 6 June 1944. Like Rommel, he committed suicide when the attempt to assassinate Hitler on 20 July 1944, of which he had knowledge, failed.

direct contact with Russia or its satellites; namely, in Germany, Austria, at Trieste and Korea.

These points of contact represent only a fraction of the vast Russian frontier with the outside world. There are open frontiers with Russia in the Balkans, Czechoslovakia and Turkey, in Persia, the Middle East and India, and there is the vast frontier with China and the frontiers in the Scandinavian peninsula. The Soviet [Union] could move in many directions in Europe or in Asia without coming into immediate conflict with any American forces whatsoever. In many of these areas, if Russia chose to advance, she would find war-weary peoples with no desire to fight. Nor are these areas covered by precise American commitments as to what we would do if Russia took the "calculated" or "miscalculated" risk of advancing, though in the specific case of Italy, as our troops withdrew, we gave Russia a hint that we would not stand idly by if Italy's independence was threatened.

Fortunately, there is no reason to believe that Russia contemplates overt military aggression. In three major wars Russia was saved by the consuming effect of great distance and the hostility of occupied peoples. Hence, Russia must well know the eventual consequences of overexpansion. And there is reason to hope that the Russian leaders do not have the military madness of a Hitler.

If Russia moves, it will be far more subtly. By bringing about the internal disintegration of the states which she wishes to incorporate, she hopes to absorb them into her direct sphere of influence without resorting to open warfare. Today Russia's major effort is directed against West Europe for today it is vulnerable. This then becomes the area for the employment of strategic American economic power. We must recognize, however, that tomorrow Russia might shift the pressure from Europe to the Middle or Far East.

Our announced policy to meet this from of aggression, in the areas which seem most immediately threatened, is to help toward building up the economic life and defensive power of threatened states to a point where these subtler Soviet methods will be ineffective. Our help is to be primarily through economic and financial aid. It is to be given to support free people who are attempting to resist subjugation.

This is the basis of the foreign policy which the United States is following today. While its wider implications may not yet be fully understood, the Congress has so far given approval to the policy in its limited application to Greece and Turkey. By voting interim relief for France, Italy, Austria, and China in the Foreign Aid Act of 1947, it has started on the way toward giving its approval to this policy as applied to the countries which are cooperating with us to realize the Marshall Plan. Thus within the means available to us, and these means have definite limitations, we stand committed to leadership in the defense of free peoples. We have adopted that policy not out of charity but for our own protection.

Just as, in 1823, we could not have carried out the Monroe Doctrine alone, so today we need strong and peace-loving friends and allies. I do not mean military allies. We should not deceive ourselves. There is not a state in Europe which does not hope to remain neutral if it can remain unoccupied in the event that Russia should move with force of arms. I mean allies to work with us with peaceful means for the maintenance of freedom.

The Marshall Plan is not merely a philanthropic program. It is an attempt, in one vitally important area of the world, to protect free institutions, because we feel that in the world today we cannot live safely if these institutions disappear elsewhere. It is a logical extension of traditional American policy, a policy for which we fought in two world wars, a policy which can be stated as simply as this: That we do not propose, if we can help it, to permit a great power, with a system incompatible with ours, to overrun Europe or Asia.

APPENDICES

Appendices

Introduction

by Allen W. Dulles
dated 7 January 1948

The purpose of this book is to present the background facts about the Marshall Plan and to put under one cover the basic documents so that the reader can easily get at the source material himself.[1]

Secretary of State George C. Marshall on June 5, 1947 called upon the nations of Europe to get together and tell us what they proposed to do so that we in the United States could determine what we would do. Since that time, sixteen European powers have put their ideas down on paper, and on this side of the water a vast amount of work has been done in trying to analyze what we could and should do about it. While the daily press has done a good job in giving us the day-by-day developments affecting the European Recovering Program, much of the important documentation which I have mentioned above is hidden away in government reports and congressional papers, which are both forbidding to the ordinary reader and hard to get at.

With persistent effort I have succeeded in corralling most of the public documentation about the Marshall Plan.[2] I call it "public" because none of it is secret – not because the public is likely to be able to get it. In this democracy of ours we persist in maintaining the most ineffective machinery for making available to the public in readable form the vast stores of

1. The documents Dulles is referring to are available to the public today, and there is thus no need to include them in this publication. They are Secretary Marshall's speech of 5 June 1947, Molotov's rejection of the Marshall Plan, summary of CEEC report, manifesto of the Cominform, summaries of the Krug, Harriman, and Nourse reports, Marshall's statement before congressional committees, Herter's Foreign Aid Bill, Foreign Aid Act of 1947, Truman's 19 December 1947 message to Congress, draft legislation submitted with Truman's message, text of U.S.–French agreement of 2 January 1948, and exchange of letters between Senator Vandenberg and the State Department.

2. Dulles, despite his many ties with the administration and his affiliation with the Council on Foreign Relations, had problems getting hold of the documents. To Frank G. Wisner of the State Department he wrote

> for the life of me I have not been able, up to the present time, to lay my hands on a single copy of the proposed legislation which I understand accompanied the President's message.... As I am doing some writing on the Marshall Plan, I have, I believe, about the most complete collection of documentation on the subject of anyone in New York, but it has been a major operation to get these documents.

See Dulles to Wisner, 23 December 1947, Allen Dulles Papers, box 31; also Dulles to Wisner, 8 January 1948, Allen Dulles Papers, box 36.

information which daily come out of the various departments of government.

Following Secretary Marshall's Harvard commencement speech, the first important source document is the statement sent us by the West European powers. It is called the Report of the Committee of European Economic Cooperation and is dated September 21, 1947. I generally refer to it as the CEEC report. Then, on October 9, 1947, came the report of J. A. Krug, secretary of the interior. This dealt with "National Resources and Foreign Aid." On October 28, 1947, there followed the report of the president's Committee of Economic Advisers, generally referred to as the Nourse report. It was entitled "The Impact of Foreign Aid Upon the Domestic Economy."

To those readers who want to be really well informed on the complexities and problems of the European Recovery Program, I recommend the report of the President's Committee on Foreign Aid, generally known as the Harriman report, which was issued on November 7, 1947 under the title of "European Recovery and American Aid." Here, in less than 300 pages, the reader has a relatively complete and a thoroughly dispassionate discussion by competent experts, most of whom have no governmental or political axes to grind. The report is well written and not so technical as to frighten the amateur. As long as the supply lasts, the government printing office will dispense it at sixty cents a copy.

Under date of November 10, 1947, the staff of the Senate Foreign Relations Committee and the House Foreign Affairs Committee prepared a most useful pamphlet, entitled "Basic Documents and Background Information," for the use of these committees. I have found this compilation of the greatest help and have made liberal use of it.

At various dates, beginning early in November and continuing through November 24, 1947, the Select Committee on Foreign Aid of the House of Representatives (the Herter committee) submitted eleven preliminary reports on various phases of the Marshall Plan. These reports deal with the situations in various of the key countries of Europe, their needs, and American availabilities, and the general principles and organization of a foreign aid program. I have found their reports of great value and have made many references to them. They constitute a most important addition to the over all documentation of the Marshall Plan.

Following Secretary Marshall's statement to the foreign relations and foreign affairs committees of the Senate and the House on November 10, 1947, which is reproduced in the appendices, President Truman on December 19, 1947, submitted a message to the Congress presenting in detail the administration's view of the European Recovery Program. Together with this message, the president submitted a lengthy memorandum prepared in the executive departments, very largely in the State Department, and entitled "An Outline of a European Recovery Program." This memorandum included a draft of the legislation proposed by the executive departments to give effect to the Marshall Plan. The president's message and the draft legislation are both included in the appendices. The report, to which I make frequent reference as the executive report, is too long to be reproduced in full. As only preliminary mimeographed copies of this report were available when this book went to press, it was not possible to give page references for the various quotations which I make from it.

This is the documentation on which the Congress will proceed to consider the form, substance, and amount of a European recovery program. It will be supplemented by oral testimony before the committees of Congress. However, by and large, the formal written case is in. The American people and the Congress, the jury of public opinion will now determine a course of action. Their decision will affect our foreign policy for many years.

New York
January 7, 1948.

Chronology of Significant Events Relating to the European Recovery Program

by Allen W. Dulles
dated 7 January 1948

1947

June 5	Secretary of State George C. Marshall makes his proposal in Harvard University commencement address.
June 14	Foreign Minister Georges Bidault invites Foreign Minister Ernest Bevin to Paris to discuss proposal.
June 17	Conference in Paris between Foreign Minister Bidault and Foreign Minister Bevin.
June 19	Invitation sent from Paris to Foreign Minister Molotov to join Messrs. Bevin and Bidault.
June 22	President Truman appoints three committees to study implications of European Recovery Plan – the Krug committee to study state of nation's resources, the Nourse committee to study the impact on our economy of aid to other countries, and the Harriman committee to advise the president on the limits within which the United States may safely and wisely plan to extend assistance.
June 23	Foreign Minister Molotov accepts invitation to Paris conference.
June 24	Poland agrees to cooperate with the Marshall Plan.
June 27	Opening of Paris conference with Messrs. Bevin, Bidault, and Molotov in attendance.
July 2	Paris conference breaks down with Molotov's opposition to any offer of economic organization for Europe.
July 3	Foreign Ministers Bevin and Bidault issue joint invitation to twenty-two European powers to meet in Paris to discuss Marshall Plan.
July 7–10	Tass, official Russian news agency, reports Poland, Yugoslavia, and Rumania cannot attend conference.
July 9	Rumania, Bulgaria, Poland, Yugoslavia refuse invitaion. Premier Klement Gottwald of Czechoslovakia flies to Moscow.

July 10	Czechoslovakian government withdraws acceptance; Hungary, Albania, and Finland send refusals.
July 12	Conference convenes in Paris with forty-eight diplomats representing sixteen nations in attendance.
July 12	Premier Klement Gottwald and Foreign Minister Masaryk of Czechoslovakia conclude a five-year trade pact with Russia.
July 22	House of Representatives establishes Select Committee on Foreign Aid (Herter committee).
September 12	French Foreign Ministry announces study of a customs union by Austria, Belgium, Britain, Denmark, France, Greece, Iceland, Italy, Ireland, Luxembourg, the Netherlands, Portugal, Rumania, and Turkey.
September 22	The Committee of European Economic Cooperation (CEEC) signs its report and transmits it to the United States government.
October 1	President Truman requests Appropriations and Foreign Relations Committees of both houses of Congress to meet promptly to consider stopgap aid.
October 6	Cominform organized at Warsaw to combat Marshall Plan.
October 7	Krug report issued.
October 22	Speaking for Cominform, General Zhdanov calls upon Communists everywhere to wreck the Marshall Plan, an instrument of American imperialism.
October 23	President Truman calls special session of Congress for November 17, 1947.
October 28	Council of Economic Advisers submits report (Nourse report) to the President.
November 6	President's Committee on Foreign Aid submits its report (Harriman report) to the president.
November 10	Senate Foreign Relations Committee and House Foreign Affairs Committee meet in joint session to receive report of Secretary of State Marshall.
November 17	Congress meets in special session.
November 15 to December 15	Council of Foreign Ministers meets in London to consider the German problem and adjourns *sine die*.

December 4	French Communists call off strikes.
December 17	Foreign Aid Act of 1947 (interim aid for Austria, China, France, and Italy) approved by the president and becomes law.
December 19	President Truman submits a message to Congress together with an "Outline of a European Recovery Program" prepared by the executive departments.
December 19	Secretary Marshall reports to the country on the breakdown of the meeting of foreign ministers.

1948

| January 2 | The American-French agreement covering interim aid signed in Paris. |
| January 6 | Second session of 80th Congress convenes. |

Index

Index

Kennan, George F., xxi, 122 n. 10, 123 n. 12
Keyserling, Leon, 56
Kipling, Rudyard, 15
Kluge, Günther von, 123
Kovács, Béla, 22 n. 3
Krock, Arthur, 90
Krug, Julius A., 54–56, 62, 129 n. 1, 130, 132, 133

Lansing, Robert, xvi
League of Nations, 1, 65, 95, 109, 119
Lend-Lease Act, 23
Lenin, 109
Lippmann, Walter, 122, 123
Lovett, Robert M., xii, xiii, xv, 31, 68 n. 7
Luxembourg, 3 n. 5, 17 n. 29, 28, 39, 46, 133

Magna Carta, 109
Malthus, Thomas Robert, 12
Manchuria, 118 n. 4
Maria Christina, queen regent of Spain, 11 n. 16
Marne, Battle of the, 13
Marshall, George C., ix, x, xi, xii, xiii, xiv, xv, xvi, xxi, xxii, 1–4, 6, 20–22, 24, 27–37, 39, 40, 43, 49, 52, 54, 58, 60, 61, 62, 65–69, 71–73, 75–78, 80, 81, 84–86, 89–97, 99, 100, 102, 104–108, 110–112, 116, 120–123, 125, 129, 130, 132–134
Marshall's Harvard commencement address, xii, 2, 6, 21, 22, 129 n. 1
Marx, Karl, 3, 109
Masaryk, Jan, 29, 133
Middle East, 11, 124
Molotov, 3, 4, 22–28, 30, 35–37, 50, 106, 109, 129 n. 1, 132
"Molotov Plan," 35
Monroe Doctrine, 118, 119, 122, 125
Mussolini, 39 n. 1

Napoleon, 13 n. 19, 118
Napoleonic wars, 8
National Resources Production Act, 86
National Advisory Council (NAC), 76
Nations Participating in Marshall Program, 28
Near East Colleges Association, xviii
Nenni, Pietro, 33
The Netherlands, xxi, 3, 5, 8, 10, 11, 13, 17, 28, 39, 45–48, 64, 69, 71, 78, 87, 106, 133
Norway, 3 n. 5, 25, 28, 39, 48, 78
Nourse, Edward G., 54, 56, 57, 62, 129 n. 1, 130, 132, 133

Office of Strategic Services (OSS), xx, xvii, xviii, 123 n. 14
Open Door, 118, 119, 122
"Operation Sunrise," xvi

Paris Peace Conference, Versailles, xvi
Patterson, Robert P., xiii, xiv n. 11, xiv
Paul, Rudolf, 29
Paxton, Joseph, 9 n. 13
Pearl Harbor, ix n. 2, xvii, 58
Pearson, Drew, 113 n. 8, 114
Pearson, Weetman (Lord Cowdray), 15, 16
Persia, 124
Petkov, Nikola Dimitrov, 22
Philippines, 12 n. 17
Phillips, Cabell, 56
Poland, xix, 2 n. 4, 25, 28, 29, 31, 34–36, 100, 106, 107, 132
Portugal, 3 n. 5, 28, 39, 45, 78, 133
Potsdam Conference, xx, 38
Pravda, 22
Preparatory Commission on the Limitations of Armaments, xvii
Puerto Rico, 12 n. 17

Rawdon-Hastings, Francis, 16
Reconstruction Finance Corporation, 72
Rhodes, Cecil, 15, 16
Ripka, Hubert (Ri[p]ka), 35
Rockefeller, John Davison, 17
Rommel, Erwin, 123
Roosevelt, Franklin D., xvii, 38 n, 39, 72 n. 10, 118 n. 3, 120
Rothschild banking house, 9
Royal Institute for International Affairs, 16 n. 19
Rumania, 25, 28, 29, 31, 34, 36, 132, 133
Rundstedt, Gerd von, 123

Scandinavian Peninsula, 124
Schacht, Hjalmar, 32
Serbia, 11 n. 15, 17 n. 29
Sherman Anti-Trust Law, 118
Soviet Union (Russia), ix, x, xviii, xx, xxi, 3–5, 9–11, 17, 21–28, 29–31, 33–38, 50, 63, 65, 69, 84, 100, 106, 108–110, 112, 116, 119, 121, 122, 123–125, 133
Spanish-American War (1898), 11, 120 n. 6
stabilization fund, 44
Stalin, 4, 24, 38, 50, 109
Stimson, Henry L., xi
Sullivan & Cromwell, xvii, xviii, xxii
Sweden, 3 n. 5, 28, 34, 39, 48, 78

137

Index

Swift, Gustavus Franklin, 17
Switzerland, x, xvi, xvii, xviii, 3, 28, 34, 39, 42, 45, 78, 117, 123

Taft, Robert A., 105
Teheran Conference, 38
Tehuantepec railway, 15
Thorez, Maurice, 32
Three Power Naval Conference, Geneva, xv
Togliatti, Palmiro, 32
Toynbee, Arnold J., 117
Trieste, 32, 124
Truman, Harry S., xviii, 31, 38 n. 39, 41, 54, 55 n. 7, 56 n. 11, 64, 65 n. 4, 66–70, 74 n. *, 75, 79, 106, 120–122, 129 n. 1, 130, 132–134
Truman Doctrine, 106, 121
Turkey, xvii, 3 n. 5, 10, 11 n. 15, 18, 28, 39, 45, 78, 106, 120, 121 n. 8, 122, 124, 133

Ukraine, 106
United Kingdom, 3 n. 5, 7–10, 13–17, 19, 21, 25–27, 38, 39, 45, 48, 52, 63, 64, 71, 83, 85, 87, 99, 103–106, 113, 119, 121
United States Steel Corporation, 17
United Nations Relief and Rehabilitation Administration (UNRRA), 63–65, 81, 105, 106

Vandenberg, Arthur H., xi, xv, 30, 68, 95, 97, 98 n. 7, 129 n. 1
Vestey family, Liverpool, 13–16
Victoria, Queen of England, 16
Vishinsky, Andrei Y., 109

War and Peace Studies project, Council on Foreign Relations, xix, 110 n. 2
Washington, George, Farewell Address, 119
Waterloo, Battle of, 13
Watt, James, 7
Wellington, Arthur Duke of, 13 n. 19
Whitney, Eli, 7
Wilhelm II, Kaiser of Germany, 11
Wendell Willkie, 3
Wilson, Woodrow, xvi, 18, 109, 119, 120
Wolff, Karl, SS General, xvii, xviii, 39
Woodrow Wilson Foundation, xvii n. 11, xviii
World Bank, 63, 64, 66, 67, 73, 76, 77, 85, 89

"X" [Kennan, George F.], 122

Yalta Conference, 38
Yovanovitch, Dragolub 22
Yugoslavia, 22, 23, 28–32, 106, 132
Zhdanov, Andrei A., 31, 84, 133